LUTHERAN VOICES

People of Purpose
40 Life Lessons from the New Testament

Robert Driver-Bishop

Augsburg Fortress

Minneapolis

PEOPLE OF PURPOSE
40 Life Lessons from the New Testament

Large-quantity purchases or custom editions of these books are available at a discount from the publisher. For more information, contact the sales department at Augsburg Fortress, Publishers, 1-800-328-4648, or write to: Sales Director, Augsburg Fortress, Publishers, P.O. Box 1209, Minneapolis, MN 55440-1209.

Library of Congress Cataloging-in-Publication Data
Driver-Bishop, Robert, 1954-
  People of purpose : 40 life lessons from the New Testament / Robert Driver-Bishop.
    p. cm.
  Includes bibliographical references.
  ISBN 0-8066-4936-4 (pbk. : alk. paper)
  1. Bible. N.T.—Biography—Study and teaching. 2. Bible. N.T.—Criticism, interpretation, etc. I. Title.
  BS2430.D75 2005
  225.9'22—dc22   2005015474

The paper used in this publication meets the minimum requirements of American National Standard for Information Sciences—Permanence of Paper for Printed Library Materials, ANSI Z329.48-1984. ♾ ™

Manufactured in the U.S.A.

08   07   06   5   6   7   8   9   10

Contents

Foreword

Christianity is more often caught than taught. Likewise, discipleship is learned through the imitation of examples and the encouragement of mentors. The problem is that many Christian churches have adopted the classroom and lecture model for teaching the faith. This might be okay if the goal is only to relay facts, but this will not result in the transformation of lives.

We have forgotten that, in previous times, most learning took place not by lecture, but by example, and not in the classroom, but through practice out in the field. This still happens today. A case in point is an apprentice carpenter who learns the trade not by listening to someone talk about building a home, but rather by watching and imitating those who are building a home. The carpenter's teachers are called master carpenters because they have achieved a status of recognized competence. Ask a nurse, pastor, scientist, or architect how they learned competence in their vocations. Chances are, they will report that they learned from a mentor while in the lab, on internship, on the hospital floor, or assisting an accomplished person with an important project.

Rodney Stark, in his book *The Rise of Christianity*, makes the point that Christianity spread rapidly in the first four centuries after Christ's death and resurrection because of the witness of the Christians through their lifestyle examples of mercy and generosity. The non-Christians observed this behavior and declared: "Look at how they love one another." Actions speak louder than words.

The beauty of *People of Purpose* by Robert Driver-Bishop is that it provides concrete examples of what it means to practice the Christian faith. These examples serve as mentors from the past. We are invited to engage these characters through reflection and discussion. We learn from them what to do and, in some cases, what not to do. Do what the Good Samaritan did. Avoid the pitfalls of the Rich Young Ruler. Be transformed as Thomas was. Here is found the way to discipleship.

People of Purpose is an excellent devotional resource, especially during the season of Lent; a chapter can be read for each of the forty days. It is well-suited to the development of a small group ministry in the congregation. Small groups have been shown to be an important tool for renewal. *People of Purpose* can serve as a handbook to discuss ministry in daily life— how we respond to God's call to serve and to witness at home, in the neighborhood, at school, in the workplace, and at church. *People of Purpose* is a helpful guide for discipleship. Jesus calls us to follow. Following Jesus is not just a theory to be studied, but it is a real life response to the love of God through Jesus Christ. For because of God's grace through Jesus, we are "marked with the cross of Christ forever, and we are claimed, gathered, and sent for the sake of the world."

Rev. Dr. Gary Wollersheim
Bishop, Northern Illinois Synod of the ELCA

Introduction

"The Bible is composed of numerous stories of men and women and their relationships with the loving God who created them. To study the lives of these individuals is meaningful and uplifting. We can learn both what to do and what to be by looking at the positive attributes of hundreds of people who fill the pages of Scripture."

—Rick Warren, *Personal Bible Study Methods*, 1982, p. 88.

Rick Warren's writings provide a practical way to grow in faith and ministry. We all need a balanced diet for health. Rick Warren prescribes a balanced spiritual life that includes worship, service, evangelism, fellowship, and discipleship. This balance is based on Jesus' greatest teachings. Together they provide an inspirational vision statement: "A Great Commitment to the Great Commandment and The Great Commission will grow a Great Church!" (*The Purpose-Driven Life*. Grand Rapids: Zondervan, 2002, p. 306)

The Great Commandment from Matthew 22:37-40 reads:
"Love the Lord your God with all your heart and with all your souls and with all your mind . . .
Love your neighbor as yourself. All the Law and the Prophets hang on these two commandments."

The Great Commission is Jesus' words to his disciples at the end of Matthew's Gospel:
"Go and make disciples of all nations, baptizing them in the name of the Father and of the Son and of the Holy Spirit, and teach them everything I have commanded you."
—Matthew 28:19-20

If you have read and discussed Rick Warren's books or engaged in a "forty days of purpose campaign," you could use this book as the basis for another forty-day emphasis in your congregation. It is also suitable for private devotion and group study and reflection.

In the mid 1970s, I was privileged to work at the highest code-word security levels of the United States Air Force Intelligence Agency. My first assignment involved taking over duties from Lieutenant Lord (it quickly circulated that a Bishop had replaced the Lord!). During the initial briefing I was told that our team provided international analysis for the White House, Pentagon, intelligence agencies, and dozens of generals. I was impressed. With a twinkle in the eye, they concluded, "So keep your reports very simple and short!"

I learned the value of extensive study, rendering an educated assessment, and delivering a succinct report. Hundreds of books about the biblical figures covered in this book have been written. This is a personal summary. Admittedly God, Jesus, the Spirit, and Satan represent more than just a single person. Hopefully this overview enables you to understand them all better. Additional resources and details about an upcoming Old Testament version of this book are provided at *www.40Lives.com*.

Special thanks go to Beth Lewis, Scott Tunseth, Scott Breyfogle, Michelle Cook, and others at Augsburg Fortress for support and encouragement; the libraries at Princeton and Luther Seminaries; Northern Illinois Diaconal Ministries; Robert Lidvall, Pastor Steve Srock, Grace Lutheran in Loves Park; and editing assistant Mariel Heinke.

This book is dedicated to my delightful daughter Anna and the Rev. Dr. Terri Driver-Bishop (loving partner in life and ministry).

To God be the Glory,
Rev. Dr. Robert Driver-Bishop

1

God the Creator

Read: Exodus 3

Background

Names are everything. They tell us about the character and quality of an individual. The phrase "In the name of God" speaks of a divine power and presence intersecting with our mortal lives.

Our relationship with God completely changed the day that Moses encountered God in the midst of the burning bush. God's name was revealed for all time as *Yahweh*. Knowing anyone's name is an important step in developing a personal relationship. Knowing this name brings us closer to God and tells us something about our Creator.

While Scripture records many names for God, *Yahweh* is the most important and sacred name of all. This name was so special that it was considered blasphemy to say it out loud in Jesus' time! It is, however, a great description of God's role in our lives. God is always active and present.

Yahweh is a unique word in the Hebrew language.

First, it is verb.

Second, it transcends all sense of time. This name incorporates the past, present, and future in just one word!

What does this mean?

When we say that God is a verb, we affirm that God is an active part of our everyday lives. The ancient Greek philosophers tried to keep their gods at a distance. These gods were on some mountain-top remote from the concerns of the everyday people. It's easy to ignore a god detached from our lives. *Yahweh* is an active part of our daily lives. God is the loving parent who cares about us. God never

1

gives up on us. God is like the loving father in the parable of the prodigal son. God cares most of all for lost children and patiently waits for the wayward child to return. As in the story of Exodus, God sees our struggles and sends help.

Our God transcends all of time. This simultaneously includes past, present, and future . . .

God of the past. This is the God who created us with a purpose. God fought the powers of darkness and chaos (Genesis 1) and brought forth light and life. Our God spoke through so many people in the Old Testament: Adam and Eve, Abraham and Sarah, Isaac, Jacob, Joseph, and their families. God heard the children of Israel cry for deliverance and called Moses. God continued to speak through the words of the priests, prophets, and sacred writings of the Holy Bible. God was fully present in the life and ministry of Jesus. This is the God of tradition and history. We never fully know "who" we are until we know "whose" we are. Centuries may pass in the blink of an eye, but God's steadfast love endures forever.

God of the present. God is present in our lives, here and now. God is an active presence in our worship, our fellowship, our discipleship, our outreach, and our service to others. God is revealed to us in many ways. We feel the presence of God as we watch a beautiful sunset, observe a mountain's majesty, or behold the miracle of a child's birth. God speaks to us through church activities, a mission event, a Bible study, a worship service, a fellowship gathering, or in a generous act of compassion.

God of the future. Jesus' last words to his disciples are known as the Great Commission. He said, "I have been given all authority in heaven and on earth! Go to the people of all nations and make them my disciples. Baptize them in the *name* of the Father, the Son, and the Holy Spirit, and teach them to do everything I have told you" (Matthew 28:18-20). Jesus concluded "I will be with you always, even until the end of the world." We are never alone. God promises unceasing care. Scientists declare that the rate of gravitational fall is a universal constant. Mathematicians maintain the formula for pi is never changing. Philosophers communicate the certainty of "death and taxes." God's love and steadfastness surpass them all. God was there yesterday, is here today, and will be with us tomorrow.

Reflections

Encountering the God of all creation is a life-changing experience. Moses met the experience with great resistance. He tried to avoid God's call with feeble excuses. Moses must have realized that the summons from God would change his life forever. God's presence in our lives changes everything. Moses was probably like so many of us who are reluctant to change.

There is the story of the man who came home one day to find his wife had hung a plaque on the wall that said "Prayer changes things." The next day he took it down. The wife was astonished and asked, "Don't you like prayer?" "Sure, I like prayer," he replied. "I just can't stand change."

Moses came to realize that God does not change things for the sake of change alone. God changes things to transform them. Changing Moses' life transformed the lives and direction of an entire nation. Moses accepted God's call, and the world was never the same. We accept God's call and our lives are transformed. With God's help, we are called to transform the world.

Reflection Questions

1. How do you know if you have a personal relationship with God? When do you feel closest to God? How does God challenge you?

2. Psalm 8 is the first psalm to praise God. Read it aloud. How does it describe your relationship with God?

3. In what ways has God initiated change in your life? How has it made a difference? How have you made a difference in the lives of others?

2
The Wise Men

Read: Matthew 2:1-12

Background

When we let God provide the right direction for our lives, amazing things can happen. The story of the Wise Men is a great example of the rewards awaiting those who follow God's purposes. In this story, the Creator used the light of a star to herald the birth of the only begotten son.

The Wise Men traveled west seeking the Christ child. They turned to King Herod, the powerful leader of Israel, looking for further directions. Herod didn't have a clue. He was not in touch with God's purposes. The temple advisors were consulted; they too were out of touch with God's plan. At last they consulted the Scriptures. They discovered the ancient prophets foretold that the Messiah would someday be born "in Bethlehem, in Judea."

These Wise Men were the first Gentiles (foreigners) to visit the newborn King. They came from faraway lands in the east. Even in birth, Jesus was the catalyst for breaking down boundaries and barriers. God's message is meant for everyone, everywhere. Dividing walls between different races, countries, and cultures are contrary to God's kingdom.

Tradition indicates that there were three wise men (probably because there were only three gifts!). Writings from the sixth century indicate their names were Caspar, Melchior, and Balthasar. Their gifts were all native to Arabia and symbolically embodied three different aspects of Jesus: his divinity, his humanity, and his kingly office.

Melchior brought frankincense, a sweet perfume from Arabia and produced near Sheba. This perfume was used in the preparation of incense and holy anointing oil (Exodus 30:34). This gift reflected Christ's high priestly office and was a pleasant offering for the Son of God.

Balthasar brought myrrh, a preservative used in anointing the dead (Exodus 30:23-33). Naomi once said, "Call me no longer Naomi, call me Mara [from the same same root word as *myrrh*], for the Almighty has dealt bitterly with me" (Ruth 1:20). Myrrh symbolized the human suffering that Jesus endured when he came into our world.

Caspar brought gold, a very rare metal in biblical times. Gold was the mark of nobility (only a king could afford it!). The Wise Men may have offered Jesus this most precious gift of ancient times, but Christ is the greatest gift the world has ever known. Jesus is the King of kings.

Reflections

The Wise Men realized that new things happen all the time with God. They trusted God and left their homes when they saw the right sign. This story teaches us several things:

The Christ child from the beginning brought a message that would unite east and west in peace. Christian nations have clashed with Arab nations for centuries, including crusades, and recent conflicts in the Persian Gulf region. From the very beginning, Jesus inspired us to heal divisions. It takes great wisdom to seek the uniting presence of God in the world today. Those who follow Christ are called to be peacemakers.

The Wise Men shared great riches with a humble child born in a stable. Many of us celebrate Christmas by only giving presents to people we know. Christmas is an opportunity to remember that God's gift of love is meant for everyone! Jesus criticized those who only cared for friends, families, and neighbors. We are called to reach out and care for the unloved, forgotten, abandoned, and undeserving, just as God reaches out for each one of us.

The Wise Men knew that God has a purpose for us all. That's why they kept watch for a sign from God. They finally saw that bright shining star to lead the way. They traveled because God held the center of their attention. God had a great plan in mind when he sent Jesus. This was a new covenant, a New Testament, a new opportunity for a closer relationship with God. We need to watch for signs from God and be willing to follow them. God's light continues to provide direction for all our lives. We need to be open to following God's plan. It's a marvelous thing to behold.

The biblical word for *wisdom* means the ability to see and follow God's will for us in the world. Wisdom requires that we look for God's purpose and then do it. Wisdom is never passive. Pursuing God's purpose is always the wisest course of action.

Reflection Questions

1. Henry Wadsworth Longfellow (1807-1882) wrote several poems about the life of Christ. In these verses from "The Three Kings," can you imagine Mary's reaction to the Wise Men? Why was her heart troubled yet comforted?

His mother, Mary of Nazareth, Sat watching beside his place of rest,
Watching the even flow of his breath,
for the joy of life and the terror of death
Were mingled together in her breast.
They laid their offerings at his feet:
The gold was their tribute to a King,
The frankincense, with its odor sweet,
was for the Priest, the Paraclete,
The myrrh for the body's burying.
And the mother wondered and bowed her head,
And sat as still as a statue of stone;
Her heart was troubled yet comforted,
Remembering what the Angel had said
Of an endless reign and of David's throne.

2. Mary understood that God's way is not always the easy way. In what manner does God continue to provide direction for your life? How do you see God's hand in your life? Are you willing to follow regardless of cost? Why?

3. How can we be peacemakers in the world? What conflicts need to be resolved? What gifts has God given us to make a difference?

3
Herod

Read: Matthew 2:13-23

Background

King Herod the Great came from a long line of Jewish royalty. As a young man he formed a political alliance with Octavian (also known as Caesar Augustus) and was rewarded with great powers throughout Israel and surrounding lands. In 40 BC the Roman Senate appointed Herod king of Israel. Herod the Great consolidated his power by killing many of the Jewish royal religious leaders (Hasmoneans) who had brought freedom to Israel during the Maccabean revolt.

Herod was very ambitious. He became a builder king and oversaw the construction of immense palace fortresses in Samaria, Jericho, Bethlehem, Jerusalem, and Masada (most of which are modern day tourist stops).

Herod also built a new temple in Jerusalem that was one of the largest worship centers of ancient times. The foundations covered a full thirty-five acres. The craftsmen used the finest marble and gold. Stones were taken from a nearby quarry called Golgotha. Some said it was so beautiful it made up for all the innocent people who Herod had killed! Herod had built a new sanctuary but left no room in his heart for God to dwell.

Herod was also a clever politician who would do absolutely anything to preserve his power. He was merciless when his own safety or position was threatened. Herod embraced the ideals of the Greco-Roman culture, but he also considered himself a messianic ruler (like King David).

When Herod was informed by the Wise Men that the "King of the Jews" was born, he became very jealous. This was a biblical name Herod sometimes claimed for himself. Rather than considering the possibility that Jesus could be God's own son, Herod viciously responded to the news by ordering the slaughter of the young innocent male children of Bethlehem (similar to Pharaoh's monstrous massacre of children in Moses' time).

Herod and Jesus are a study of contrasts:

Herod was the royal king of the land; Jesus was poor and born in a manger.

Herod had all earthly power and might; Jesus was a helpless baby.

Herod used his position in greedy and cruel ways; Jesus empowered others with love.

Herod was crafty and sly; Jesus was trustworthy.

Herod wanted to be an all-powerful leader; Jesus is the King of kings and Lord of all Creation.

Herod executed three of his sons and his favorite (Jewish) wife during fits of paranoiac rage. Caesar Augustus remarked that it was safer to be a pig in Israel than one of Herod's sons. Ultimately disease destroyed his body just as greed and power and lust had destroyed his soul. He never found the love, security, and meaning in life he was seeking. This builder king ultimately lacked a spiritual foundation.

Reflections

King Herod the Great is a somber example of someone whose purpose in his life is misdirected. In some ways he had it all; in other ways he had nothing. Everyone's life is driven by something. Herod was driven by fear, greed, and earthly power. He had everything by worldly standards and yet he never found true happiness.

One wonders why people call Alexander or Herod "Great" when they spent their lives conquering and oppressing other people. They may have been powerful in the eyes of the world, but they led unfulfilled lives in the sight of God.

Lord Acton, a history professor at Cambridge, wrote that "power corrupts, and absolute power corrupts absolutely." Herod placed his ultimate faith in power. His purpose in life was to build himself up by tyrannizing others. He was a slave to his own desires and ambition.

Herod sought security in possessions. He had everything by the world's standards and yet had nothing by God's criteria. He ended up insecure and filled with fear. His life had no meaning because he ignored God's purposes.

None of our accomplishments ever earn us salvation or a special place in God's kingdom. Our acts of loving kindness flow as expressions of appreciation for the love that God shares with us. We don't seek to rule others. We seek to be part of the kingdom that lasts forever. Earthly domains come and go, but God's kingdom lasts forever.

We trust in God's guidance but recognize that we can make choices that change the path we walk and the life we lead. Herod made choices that brought pain to many, including himself. May we seek to make life-giving choices.

Reflection Questions

1. Aurelius Clemens Prudentius (AD 348-413) was a Christian poet who wrote about Herod's killing of the innocents in Bethlehem. What use was Herod's violence?

All hail, ye little martyr flowers, Sweet rosebuds cut in dawning hours!
When Herod sought the Christ to find ye fell as bloom before the wind.
First victims of the martyr bands, with crowns and palms in tender hands,
Around the very altar, gay, and innocent, ye seem to play.
What profited this great offense? What use was Herod's violence?
A Babe survives that dreadful day, And Christ is safely borne away.

2. People who don't know their purposes are often driven by their own desires. This causes stress, disease, and conflict. Why is it so difficult to admit our limitations and trust more in God?

3. The temple built by Herod was completely destroyed shortly after completion. What things in our lives are only temporary? Which things will last forever?

4

Mary

Read: Luke 1:26-56

Background

She has been known by many names including the Queen of Angels, Holy Mother, Blessed Mother, Queen of Peace, Queen of Heaven, Virgin Mary, Virgin of Guadalupe, Miriam of Nazareth, Daughter of Zion, Second Eve, Queen of all Saints, *Theotokos* (Mother of God), Handmaid of the Lord, *Mater Dolorosa* (sorrowful Mother), Model of Faith, *Mater Gloriosa* (Glorious Mother), and the Mother of Jesus.

The ten scriptural references regarding Mary are known as the "Evangelical Virtues." They are as follows: Most **Pure** (Matthew 1:18, 20, 23; Luke 1:24, 34), Most **Prudent** (Luke 2:19, 51), Most **Humble** (Luke 1:48), Most **Faithful** (Luke 1:45; John 2:5), Most **Devout** (Luke 1:46-47; Acts 1:14), Most **Obedient** (Luke 1:38, 2:21-22, 27), Most **Poor** (Luke 2:7), Most **Patient** (John 19:25), Most **Merciful** (Luke 1:39, 56), Most **Sorrowful** (Luke 2:35).

She is second only to Jesus as Christianity's most popular subject of religious poetry and art. The Koran speaks of Mary as the virginal mother of Jesus. The Roman Catholic Church has some twenty-three separate festival days to celebrate her life. During the crisis of the fourteenth century Black Plague, Mary was venerated in popular piety as mediator of the mercy of Christ. Among the many popular devotions that developed during that time was the rosary (a string of beads originally consisting of 150 Hail Mary's in tribute to the 150 Psalms).

Some of the most beautiful cathedrals in the world are named after Mary (including Reims, Chartres, Rouen, Amiens, Nîmes, Evreux, Paris—Notre-Dame, Bayeux, Séez, and Toulon). Our Lady of Peace (Ivory Coast) is the world's largest church accommodating two hundred thousand people.

-Christopher Columbus showed his devotion to Mary by naming his flagship Santa María. The crew offered daily prayers to Mary for guidance and protection while seeking the New World.

Martin Luther's commentary on the "Magnificat" states "the Gospels praise Mary by calling her the Mother of Jesus" (eight times). Later Luther preached, "[she is the] highest woman and the noblest gem in Christianity after Christ. . . . She is nobility, wisdom, and holiness personified. We can never honor her enough. Still honor and praise must be given to her in such a way as to injure neither Christ nor the Scriptures" (*Christmas Sermon*, 1531).

The reformed leader Zwingli wrote, "I esteem immensely the Mother of God," and "The more the honor and love of Christ increases among us, so much the esteem and honor given to Mary should grow."

Reflections

So what can we make of this young teenage girl who was asked by God to bear the Savior of the world? We know she was from very humble beginnings. What she lacked in earthly possessions, she made up for in God's special gift of wisdom. Early church leaders like Augustine maintained that wisdom "pertains to the knowledge of eternal things" and Clement of Alexander said wisdom was "knowledge of things both human and divine." Fittingly, the Old and New Testament words for wisdom are both feminine (*Sophia* and *Pneuma*).

Wisdom does not come from simply reading books, acquiring knowledge, or growing older. Wisdom is a gift from God that enables us to see and understand God's presence in the world about us. True wisdom enables us to understand God's purposes for us.

It takes wisdom to appreciate Mary's song known as "The Great Magnificat" (see p. 12). It speaks of the Lord's coming for all God's people. The overthrow of the tyrant does not come through the violent rebellion of the oppressed but through God's transformation of the world. The humble child born in Bethlehem changes the world for God's good. This is a peace that surpasses the world's understanding.

We are called to be like Mary. Mary understood what it meant to be a servant of the Lord. She understood that she was blessed when she shared God's blessing with others. Ironically the name *Mary* means "one who is obstinate" or "never changes." That just goes to show us that God can transform things and make them better. Mary was chosen to be the mother of Jesus, the world's greatest change agent. Lives are always changing by his everlasting message.

Reflection Questions

1. Consider the words of Mary's "Magnificat" (Luke 1:46-55). How does the birth of Jesus compare with the rule of Herod the Great?

My soul magnifies the Lord, and my spirit rejoices in God my Savior,
*   for he has looked with favor on the lowliness of his servant.*
Surely, from now on all generations will call me blessed; for the
*   Mighty One has done great things for me, and holy is his name.*
His mercy is for those who fear him from generation to generation.
He has shown strength with his arm;
he has scattered the proud in the thoughts of their hearts.
He has brought down the powerful from their thrones, and lifted up
*   the lowly;*
He has filled the hungry with good things, and sent the rich away
*   empty.*
He has helped his servant Israel, in remembrance of his mercy,
*   according to the promise he made to our ancestors,*
*   to Abraham and to his descendants forever.*

2. Mary's "Magnificat" speaks of three revolutions: scattering the proud (social change), exalting the humble (moral change), and feeding the hungry (economic change). How do these apply to our lives as Christians today? As a church?

3. Mary's dedication and devotion is an example for all eternity. What lessons can she still teach us?

5
Joseph

Read: Matthew 1:18-25

Background

Joseph was engaged to Mary. According to the custom of the day, engagement was a serious commitment that was just as important as marriage. If something happened to the intended husband during the engagement, the woman would legally have been considered a widow.

When Joseph, "being a righteous man and unwilling to expose her to public disgrace" (Matthew 1:19), found out that Mary was expecting a child, he sought to handle the matter in a quiet way. He did not want to hurt Mary but wanted to take appropriate action. That night God spoke to Joseph in his dreams and assured him Jesus was God's only begotten son. Joseph was entrusted with caring for the mother and child. He married Mary and took care of the child as his own.

The Gospels indicate that Joseph was a humble, kindly, considerate, and generous person. As a conscientious father he would have passed on the carpenter's trade to Jesus. More importantly, Joseph demonstrated what it meant to be a father:

Joseph was the obedient servant of the Lord who followed God's instruction to care for the mother and child, as revealed in a dream.

Joseph safeguarded his family by taking them to Egypt to protect the child from a violent and wicked king.

Joseph worshiped the Lord and followed God's purposes for his life. Joseph took Jesus to the temple for dedication.

Joseph cared for Jesus. He moved the family to Nazareth when they returned from Egypt so they would be safe from Jerusalem threats.

Reflections

Life is a special test and trust. Joseph was given the responsibility of caring for the Christ child. Joseph was kindhearted and responsible. One of the worst things in all creation is a father who does not provide for his children (1 Timothy 5:8). The inverse would suggest that one of the greatest things in all creation is a loving and responsible father. A loving father always cares.

Joseph's care for his family was clearly influenced by his faith. Joseph was active in the family's faith life. God spoke to him in dreams. He took his child to the temple for dedication, offered sacrifices, and participated in the religious celebrations in Jerusalem.

Some parents just drop their children off at church saying, "It will be good for them." They stay home or eat in local restaurants while their children are nurtured with the word of God. Their lives state, "do as I say and not as I do." These parents miss the great opportunity of growth together as a whole family of God.

There is nothing better than a family that worships and follows God together. Joseph was the type of parent who made all the difference in the world. Joseph listened to God and saved the family in a time of crisis. Joseph's faith helped bring salvation to the world. Joseph was not a man of many words. He showed devotion for God and family with his loving actions.

We are all given special responsibilities in our lives. Sometimes it is the faithful caring for our children and families. Other times we are called to care for others. With God's help we respond and follow the model set for us by the Holy First Family.

Like Joseph, Jesus had a special place in his heart for children. One day when the disciples denied children access, Jesus rebuked them and said, "Let the little children come to me, and do not stop them; for it is to such as these that the kingdom of heaven belongs" (Matthew 19:14). Another time Jesus warned that it would be better to be weighed down with a heavy stone and cast into the sea than to harm one of God's children (Matthew 18:6).

Renowned Christian scholar Jaroslav Pelikan shared the story of hearing his eight-year-old daughter sing, "Jesus loves me, this I know, for the Bible tells me so." He reflected that the lyrics of the song did not really fit the child's experience. She had not read the Bible. She knew that Jesus loved her because her mother, her father, her Sunday school teacher, her pastor, and others in the Christian community had told her so. Only later would she come into contact with the Bible.

We have an obligation to care for all God's children. This takes place in the home, at church, Sunday school, vacation Bible school, schools, community centers, sports, after-school programs, medical facilities, judicial systems, social ministries, foster care, orphanages, homeless shelters, world hunger programs, missions, and many other ministries.

The name *Joseph* means, "may God add children." Let us remember this dedicated servant of the Lord every time we help a child. One of the greatest purposes of our lives is to care for God's children. God enables us to care for all children, for to such belongs the kingdom of heaven.

Reflection Questions

1. Joseph cared for a child who was not his own. In what ways can we share God's love with children in need in our community? Our nation? Our world?

2. How did Joseph come to see life from God's view? How do we put ourselves in a position to see this view?

3. How is our character built by unexpected tests in our lives? How is the character of our church built by unexpected tests? How does trust in God make a difference?

6

John the Baptist

Read: John 1:6-34

Background

John the Baptist was a prophet who arrived proclaiming God's message. Israel had not seen a prophet in some four hundred years. The role of prophets is often misunderstood. Prophets did not place a heavy emphasis on predicting the future. They were primarily people who spoke God's message openly to others.

John was God's messenger. He was concerned about preparation and led a very disciplined life. From birth he was dedicated to be God's special servant. We discover from the story of Zechariah and Elizabeth that he was probably a "Nazarite." These were people who made a special commitment of spiritual discipline. Samson, the prophet Samuel, and the Apostle Paul all made Nazarite vows.

The "vow of the Nazarite" is described in Numbers 6:1-27. It was a voluntary pledge by which people were consecrated to the Lord. During this time of separation, the Nazarite was bound by three absolute restrictions:
  • They could not consume anything derived from the grapevine, including all alcohol (v. 4).
  • No razor could be used on their head. Their hair grew long (v. 5).
  • They could not go near a dead body. They even avoided family funerals (v. 6-8).

John was a character bigger than life itself. He wore clothes of camel skin and leather. His diet was locusts and wild honey. He lived off the land and was not given to fickle fashions. On the banks of the Jordan River he spoke with a booming voice and taught repentance, which means a complete change of "heart" or "life direction."

John the Baptist's ministry prepared the way of the Lord. He summoned everyone to a life of righteousness. His emphasis was celebrating the positive moral standards of God. He condemned the wrongdoers and challenged them to follow a higher standard, a closer walk with God. John sought to cleanse the nation.

John also shared the special gift of baptism, a traditional Hebrew ceremony for the cleansing of sins. This baptism enabled people to have a right relationship with God and others. John's baptism by water also helped prepare people for the Savior's spiritual baptism.

The Gospels make it clear that John was not the messiah nor the light of the world. He was a witness to the light. John stated, "I baptize you with water for repentance, but one who is more powerful than I is coming after me; I am not worthy to carry his sandals" (Matthew 3:11). This statement is an indication of just how great John considered Jesus to be.

King Herod Antipas, son of Herod the Great, later imprisoned John for criticizing his scandalous marriage to his brother's ex-wife. John's actions were compared to Elijah's courage when he condemned King Ahab and Queen Jezebel's corruption. Neither prophet was frightened of the mighty rulers of their day. Herod's wife, Herodias, was offended by John and plotted revenge against him. She encouraged her very own daughter to seduce (her husband) Herod with a sensual dance to obtain a deadly promise. John was executed. Jesus remarked, "I tell you, among those born of women no one is greater than John; yet the least in the kingdom of God is greater than he" (Luke 7:28).

Reflections

John teaches us the importance of setting priorities in our lives. God warns us not to get too attached to the ways of the world. This world is not our home. We are only here for a short time and should use that time for accomplishing God's will and preparing ourselves to spend an eternity with God.

John also teaches us the importance of spiritual separation. We don't all have to move to the desert to make appropriate choices in our lives. John understood that success in God's kingdom is different from the ways of the world. At times we need to distance ourselves from those things that would separate us from God. We can make the right choices in our lives concerning friends, activities, music, movies, television, and other forms of entertainment. What would Jesus do?

We can be selective about our food and drink. John ate healthy food and cut himself off from those things in his life he considered a temptation. Certain things can be like a poison to our bodies. Our bodies, minds, and spirits are special gifts from God. We need to protect and care for them.

A divine irony about the ministry of John the Baptist was that in spite of teaching us about the benefits of separating ourselves from the ways of the world, he shared with us that special gift that binds us together. Baptism is that special event by which we are cleansed and united with others. We become brothers and sisters together as the family of God.

God calls us into community to share communion's common cup and to communicate the gospel of Christ with all God's children.

Reflection Questions

1. Charles Coffin, writer of this famous hymn, was denied a Christian burial due to a human disagreement about "God's grace." How can we prepare to hear Christ's message?

On Jordan's banks the Baptist's cry
Announces that the Lord is nigh;
Come, then, and hearken, for he brings
Glad tidings from the King of kings!
Then cleansed be every life from sin;
Make straight the way for God within.
Prepare we in our hearts a home
Where such a mighty Guest may come. (1736)

2. What does your baptism mean to you? How is baptism both an event and a way of living?

3. John showed great courage. How do we reveal the courage of our convictions? How do we speak out in our words and our deeds? Is anyone listening?

7
Jesus Christ

Read: John 1:1-18

Background

Jesus came to earth so we could fully understand God's glory. The word *glory* has been interpreted as "greatness" or "magnificence." Speaking to God in the High Priestly Prayer (John 17), Jesus asked that God's glory be seen in all that he said and did. This included his death on the cross.

The titles "Son of God" and "Son of Man" were titles also used by Alexander the Great and Julius Caesar. Both were born under special heavenly signs and preposterously claimed to be the world's saviors. They dedicated their lives to violence, power, enslaving, and stealing from others. Alexander sacrificed his life in a futile quest for power and greed. Modern scholars maintain Caesar willingly sacrificed his life for the power of Rome. Ultimately both failed because they were self-centered saviors.

Jesus was born under a heavenly sign and gave new meaning to those titles. Jesus spent his life loving others, empowering people, proclaiming freedom, and giving away heavenly treasures. Jesus sacrificed himself for all of us. His glorious life continues to transform lives even today. Jesus is the lasting victor because he is the God-centered savior.

At some point in our lives we realize that the *way of the world* is about *selfishly* seeking power and possessions. The *way of Christ* is *selflessly* empowering others and sharing God's gifts. That is God's magnificent way. God gave us the "gift of life" as an "act of love." In the same manner God shared Jesus with us as a gift of love. This is a New Testament (a new covenant, a new relationship). Jesus brings us the gift of new life with God.

Reflections

Names bring us closer to one another. A name gives us permission to make claims upon each other. Names provide a sacred intimacy. We share our names with those who have a special claim on us. The name *Jesus* means, "God is my salvation." In Jesus, we discover our salvation. He is our beautiful Savior. We are saved from those things that separate us from God and from one another.

Through Jesus we meet God. Knowing Jesus enables us to communicate with God. Knowing Jesus enables God to communicate with us. Jesus is the living "Word" of God. Jesus shared God's message in his birth, life, teachings, miracles, suffering, death, and resurrection. We need to share God's message in all that we say and do. When we worship, serve, witness, love God's family, and grow in Christ, we share God's glory and love with others.

Some scholars treat Jesus as just a great teacher who had a significant impact on history. They examine small details but miss the big picture. Miracles are all around us. Life and love are miracles. Believing in Jesus is an affirmation that God can be a part of our everyday lives. Something inside us seeks the presence of the divine. We invite Jesus into our lives because we have a desire to partake of "the holy" on a regular basis. We want to be closer to God.

We have the Gospels of Matthew, Mark, Luke, and John to guide us in our daily walk with God. The word *gospel* is from the Old English meaning "good news." "Gospel" is a translation of the Greek word *evangelion* which means, "to share the **good news** with others." This gospel is not just any "good news." **This is the best news ever!** It brings us the greatest freedom the world has ever known. We are no longer slaves to the ways of the world but free to follow God's way. When we accept God's message of salvation, we want to share it with others. It's impossible to keep something that great to ourselves!

Non-believers sometimes expect Christians to be perfect. It's simply not possible to be perfect. That's why we all need a Savior. It is possible for us to share signs of God's grace, God's compassion, God's acceptance, God's love, and God's forgiveness. In those moments others can catch a glimpse of Jesus alive and living in our hearts. In those moments the world catches a glimpse of the divine. Salvation is at hand.

Jesus is the great paradox of all history. He was born so that he might die. He died so that we might have life. Jesus called ordinary people and made them his Holy Apostles. He took regular water and made it a holy gift of cleansing and the mark of the family of God. He took common bread and wine and made them sacred signs of his sacrificial body and blood. He makes common things divine. He welcomes us and makes us his holy people.

Jesus cared greatly for the lost and forgotten. He said the kingdom of God belongs to the children. He shared his teachings with those who were marginalized in his day. He challenged the powerful and mighty with weapons of peace and compassion. Jesus transforms the world and changes lives. Jesus calls us to follow him and reach out to others. This transformation is a glorious sign of God's love.

Reflection Questions

1. Here are some biblical names for Jesus. Which are your favorites? Why?

Lord of All—Acts 10:36, **Son of God**—John 1:34, **Word of Life**—1 John 1:1, **Prince of Life**—Acts 3:15, **Bread of Life**—John 6:35, **Lamb of God**—John 1:29, **Prince of Peace**—Isaiah 9:6, **Good Shepherd**—John 10:11, **Light of the World**—John 8:12, **Rabbi, Son of God**—John 1:49, **King of Kings**—Revelation 19:16, **Word of God**—Revelations 19:13, **Image of God**—2 Corinthians 4:4, **Wonderful Counselor**—Isaiah 9:6, **Resurrection and Life**—John 11:25, **Chief Cornerstone**—Ephesians 2:20, **Lord God Almighty**—Revelation 15:3, **Head of the Church**—Ephesians 1:22, **Only Begotten Son**—John 1:18, **Alpha and Omega**—Revelation 1:8, **Shepherd and Bishop of Souls**—1 Peter 2:25, **Author and Finisher of Our Faith**—Hebrews 12:2

2. Many historians concur that Jesus is the greatest change agent in history. How has Jesus changed history? How does Jesus Christ change people's lives today? How has he changed your life?

3. What makes Jesus the center of a person's life? How is he your Savior?

8

Zechariah and Elizabeth

Read: Luke 1:5-22

Background

Worship involves an act of complete surrender to God. We do not worship for our own benefit. We worship to please God. During worship we do not pray "*my* will be done" but "God's will be done." Worship is about completely surrendering to God's message and God's way of doing things.

This story opens with Zechariah involved in worship but not really engaged. Zechariah belonged to the twenty-four families who were the special "sons of Aaron and the priestly class." On a rotating basis, a priest was chosen from each family to tend to the holy altar located in the most sacred space of the temple. One day, while Zechariah was carrying out this privileged task, the Archangel Gabriel appeared and announced the good news that Zechariah's wife Elizabeth would have a son.

Zechariah and Elizabeth were an older couple with no children. Their story was similar to Abraham and Sarah (Genesis 16), Isaac and Rebecca (Genesis 25), Jacob and Rachel (Genesis 30), Samson's parents (Judges 13), and Elkanah and Hannah (1 Samuel 1). God gave them each children. For many years Zechariah and Elizabeth had prayed for a child. The bearing of children was considered a great blessing. Barrenness was considered by some to be a tragedy and disgrace.

Zechariah did not believe the angel Gabriel. It's not surprising that even a priest in the holy sanctuary would doubt God's messenger. It's human nature to doubt God's power. Zechariah forgot the true nature of worship, which focuses on surrendering to God's purposes for our lives. Zechariah prayed in the temple but did not believe when those prayers were answered.

It's probably an understatement to say that the Archangel Gabriel was not pleased with Zechariah's response. He was punished and could not speak because of his unbelief.

Zechariah remained mute until after his son was born. Eight days later (according to the custom), the child was presented at the temple. During the ceremony of dedication, the child received his name. The temple authorities assumed the child would be named after his father, but Elizabeth said, "No, his name is John" (Luke 1:60). Zechariah agreed by writing on a tablet "His name is John" (which means "God has been gracious"). Suddenly Zechariah could speak, and he sang a beautiful hymn of praise (*see p. 24*).

Zechariah had spent nine months listening to God, and finally he believed God's message. His son was to be a prophet. John's life would be a living act of worship. John would boldly proclaim a message of preparation of the world's salvation.

Reflections

Zechariah started out a privileged priest and ended up a humble servant of God. Just because someone has a special position in a church does not mean they always have their lives and faith in order. We are all sinners and saints at the same time.

Zechariah's story reveals that worship needs to be all about God. We come to worship to praise and honor God, not ourselves. We come to worship to hear God's message. We give God pleasure when we listen and obey.

Elizabeth, however, was obedient to God. When her cousin Mary came to visit (called the Visitation), Elizabeth did not put up objections or raise questions. She demonstrated her devotion with the words: "Blessed are you among women, and blessed is the fruit of your womb. And why has this happened to me, that the mother of my Lord comes to me? For as soon as I heard the sound of your greeting, the child in my womb leaped for joy. And blessed is she who believed that there would be a fulfillment of what was spoken to her by the Lord" (Luke 1:42-45). Scripture indicates she sang these words with great joy!

Zechariah's transformation came when he was forced to listen all the time, day after day, week after week, and month after month. We bring pleasure to God when we obediently listen and follow God's purpose for our lives. Zechariah finally got the message. His hymn identifies John's work as part of God's promises and the saving work of Jesus Christ.

Let's remember the strong faith of Elizabeth when we worship. Her name means "God is my witness." She demonstrated complete devotion to the mighty acts of God. Elizabeth is a living witness to the Lord of all Creation. Together Elizabeth and Zechariah teach us there's a time for silence and a time for praise.

Reflection Questions

1. How can we listen to God in our everyday lives? Do you have a planned listening time for God? What would such a plan look like?

2. How does a lack of faith make us mute sometimes? How can we strengthen our own faith?

3. Read this portion of Zechariah's hymn of praise. Why did the world need a savior? What is the "way of peace"?

And you, child, will be called the prophet of the Most High; for you will go before the Lord to prepare his ways, to give knowledge of salvation to his people by the forgiveness of their sins. By the tender mercy of our God, the dawn from on high will break upon us, to give light to those who sit in darkness and in the shadow of death, to guide our feet into the way of peace.

—*The Benedictus,* Luke 1:68-79

9
Jairus

Read: Mark 5:21-43

Background

Here we have two healing stories intertwined. First there's the story of Jairus' daughter. Jairus was a rich and very influential man, head of the local synagogue. He came to Jesus in desperation. His daughter was at the point of death. The heart-broken father threw himself at Jesus' feet and begged for help.

This event drew a great crowd. The respectable synagogue leader was humbling himself for his daughter's sake. The crowd followed to see what happened next. A poor sick woman took advantage of the commotion and touched the fringe of Jesus' robe. This woman was also desperate. She had given all her money to doctors (over a twelve-year period) to no avail.

The woman was at the end of her rope. She was too embarrassed to ask Jesus for help. She had severe menstrual hemorrhaging. According to Jewish law, her sickness made her ritually unclean. She wasn't rich and influential like Jairus. She just reached out and hoped God would help. She was immediately healed. God smiled.

Jesus realized something happened and sought the woman out. He delayed seeing Jairus' daughter to care for this other child of God. The woman fell at his feet (like Jairus) shaking with fear and admitted to what she had done. According to religious laws of the day, her touch made Jesus unclean, but Jesus was not upset. He lovingly told her "Daughter, your faith has made you well; go in peace, and be healed of your disease" (Mark 5:21).

Jesus declared her a member of God's family when he called her "daughter." Her trust in God bound them together. Jesus was not concerned about any human rules of contamination. Previously

Jesus had touched and healed a leper. God's healing power breaks down the barriers mere mortals construct in God's name.

Men arrived to tell Jairus his daughter was dead and that Jesus should be sent away. Jairus' daughter would never grow up to be a blessed woman of God. Jesus ignored their words and told Jairus, "do not fear, only believe." Once again, Jairus trusted Jesus.

They completed the journey to the home. A crowd gathered to mourn the loss of the child. Jesus confronted the people saying, "Why do you make a commotion and weep? The child is not dead but sleeping." The crowd scornfully laughed at Jesus. They thought they knew better. In that moment they displayed disrespect for Christ and the power of God to change things.

Jesus ignored the naysayers. He took Peter, James, John, and the parents into the house. Jesus was in the presence of those who trusted him. Jesus placed his healing hands on the girl and commanded her to get up. At once she rose and was able to walk. The parents and disciples were astonished. Jesus could both heal and share the gift of new life. Jesus then thoughtfully tended to the child's needs and saw that she was nourished.

Reflections

In this story, Jesus heals two people on opposite ends of the socio-economic scale. The unnamed woman was left impoverished because of her disease. She had given away all that she had to ineffective healers with empty promises. Jairus' daughter lived in a family of power, possessions, and prominence. All fell humbly at the feet of Jesus.

Jairus expressed the confidence that Jesus could "save" his little girl. The poor women's faith "saved her." The use of the word "save" in both cases anticipates a change, a miracle. Others would use this same word when Jesus was on the cross. Some scribes and Pharisees mocked the crucified Jesus (just like the merciless mourners in this story). They challenged Jesus to "save" himself, saying, "he saved others but cannot save himself" (Mark 15:31).

Jairus' story reveals two things. His mind and spirit were open to God's intervention in his life. He was willing to let God be God. He did not predetermine the extent of God's power. Jairus demonstrated total trust in God and a complete love for his daughter. Jairus' devotion mirrors God's love for all of us.

The interruption caused by the impoverished woman raised no objections from Jairus. He was patient. He listened to Christ's admonitions to "have faith." We should be willing to have that same level of patience and trust in God. God is pleased when we have complete trust.

This story has great significance in the New Testament. It's the only miracle story where just Peter, James, and John accompanied Jesus. These three were also with Jesus at the Transfiguration (his final preparation for his journey to Jerusalem) and in the Garden of Gethsemane where he spent his final hours praying to God. All three events are about trusting and following God's purposes.

The name *Jairus* means, "Whom God shows the way." This miracle story shows a great way. Jairus loved his family. He humbled himself and trusted God to do marvelous things. He was patient and understood many needs had to be met on the journey. He did not listen to those who mocked Jesus. He made up his own mind. He had faith in Jesus. He and his family were "saved" from a great loss. The daughter rose and was nourished in this story. So are we.

Reflection Questions

1. What was Jesus' reaction to the woman who sought healing without permission? What people are seeking help from us? What is our response?

2. Jesus shared special events with his trusted followers. Have you (or someone you know) ever had a special encounter with Christ? What happened?

3. G. K. Chesterton wrote about human weakness in search of God's health and strength. How do scorn and pride distance us from God?

O God of earth and altar, bow down and hear our cry.
Our earthly rulers falter, Our people drift and die;
The walls of gold entomb us, the swords of scorn divide,
Take not thy thunder from us, but take away our pride. (1906)

10

Caiaphas

Read: John 11:47-57

Background

It's difficult to understand Caiaphas without first considering the high priest Annas, who established a dynasty that ruled Jewish temple life for decades. After Herod the Great died there was a leadership vacuum in Israel. Rome reluctantly accepted the priests as leaders. Rome listened to anyone who sent them enough money. Caesar Augustus personally appointed Annas as leader. Many considered Annas more powerful than Pontius Pilate.

This high priest controlled the center of worship at the temple, along with all monies and the work of twenty thousand priests. Eight members of Annas' family eventually held the supreme office of high priest (Annas, five sons, a grandson, and Caiaphas, his son-in-law).

Caiaphas had simply married the boss's daughter. Even though Annas was retired, he was still the power behind the priestly throne that controlled political and religious events throughout Israel. Caiaphas may have been just a caretaker entrusted with maintaining the status quo until Annas' family could resume control.

Jesus disrupted things by driving the moneychangers from the temple. Jesus was clearly a big threat to Caiaphas. It was all about money! The tables used by the moneychangers were called "the booths of Annas." Modern archeology reveals that some priests had the richest homes in Jerusalem.

One wonders why Caiaphas even bothered to have a trial. From the offset we are told that he illegally planned to arrest Jesus and kill him (Matthew 26:4). Caiaphas was obviously more interested in getting rid of Jesus than in providing proper process. He invoked the term "God's Law" while he imposed his own version of human justice.

Caiaphas may have considered himself a righteous man because he was protecting established ways, especially the customs and practices that had become part of the temple scene. Unfortunately he missed the heart of worship. Caiaphas demanded that others obey certain laws and customs, but he missed the meaning of true obedience to God.

Caiaphas showed he had no scruples regarding his treatment of Jesus. An independent source (Josephus) indicates that there were many improprieties regarding Jesus' trial: Tradition dictated the accused must be afforded a public hearing; Jesus was not. It was illegal to try a capital charge at night; Jesus was tried at night. It was illegal for Caiaphas to encourage a prisoner to convict himself; he did. It was illegal to charge a man when the witnesses disagreed; which they did.

Later Caiaphas would continue his persecution of Christ's followers. Twice he presided over the examinations of the apostles regarding their preaching in the temple. On the advice of Gamaliel he ordered that they be beaten, warned, and released (rather than killed). He presided at the trial of Stephen and approved his subsequent stoning. He commissioned Saul with letters of authority to persecute Christians as far as Damascus.

Reflections

During the trial of Jesus, Caiaphas had shouted, "You know nothing at all" (John 11:49). Despite being the key religious leader of his time, despite talking directly with Jesus, despite the power of the resurrection, and despite witness of the apostles, Caiaphas just never got it. He loved power and position. He loved the established order. He just neglected to follow God.

For Caiaphas, the end (getting rid of Jesus) justified the means. How often do we do the same? How often do we ignore God's commands while protecting what we want? Though he accused Jesus of blasphemy, Caiaphas was the one who took God's name in vain. A priest is called to be a mediator between God and the people. Caiaphas betrayed his sacred duty.

Worship is our joyous response to the blessings and promises of God. The heart of true worship is about surrender to God. Caiaphas and Annas were upset because Jesus had upset the moneychanging tables in the temple. Jesus taught that we cannot serve both God and money. These temple leaders were serving a false god.

History teaches that those who surrender to God are sometimes asked to do unpopular, new, or unexpected things. The true test of God's presence in our endeavors is the way we work and not what we accomplish. Many considered Jesus a heretic, a troublemaker, and, ultimately, a failure on the cross. In God's kingdom, Jesus overturns all expectations. In becoming a servant of all, he showed that he was the true way, truth, and life.

Reflection Questions

1. Consider these verses from Psalm 35. Why do the wicked persecute the righteous?

Malicious witnesses rise up; they ask me about things I do not know.
They repay me evil for good; my soul is forlorn. . . .
But at my stumbling they gathered in glee,
they gathered together against me;
ruffians whom I did not know tore at me without ceasing;
they impiously mocked more and more, gnashing at me with their teeth.
How long, O Lord, will you look on?
Rescue me from their ravages, my life from the lions!

2. What in your life do you try to protect? How are your actions in line with your faith?

3. For you, what is the heart of worship? What draws you away from this true center? What draws you closer?

11

Matthew

Read: Matthew 9:9-13

Background

While we know very little about the disciple Matthew, Clement of Alexandria does tell us he was a vegetarian! We do, however, know quite a bit about his profession. He was a "publican," a civil servant employed to collect Roman taxes from his own countrymen.

The Romans were very clever. They hired local people to do the dirty business of collecting taxes for them—people who didn't mind collecting vast sums of money from their own neighbors. The privilege of collecting taxes went to the highest bidder. This often led to greed and corruption. These publicans were generally considered unclean and were not allowed to worship in the temple.

Matthew worked in Capernaum, located on the main Roman highway to Damascus. The name *Capernaum* probably comes from the Greek word for "custom house." The town was a busy harbor trafficking in fish, fruits, produce, eastern silks, and spices. Capernaum tax collectors were very busy and were quite wealthy. Matthew may have collected taxes from fishermen like Peter, Andrew, James, and John and carpenters like Joseph and Jesus.

One day Jesus passed by and simply said, "Follow me." Matthew rose and followed. Jesus did not need to ask him a second time. Matthew may have been ready for a change. Possibly he realized that this was the offer of a lifetime (and beyond). Matthew found out that those who are willing to lose everything obtain the riches of a real friendship with God.

Mark and Luke identify Matthew's original name as "Levi." The name signifies he was probably descended from the tribe of

31

Levi that was set aside to serve the Lord (Deuteronomy 8:9). They were commanded to have no possessions because the Lord was their only inheritance. Levi (Matthew) was finally living up to his family's name.

After Matthew was called, he wanted to share his good fortune with his former colleagues. He threw a banquet for a large gathering of tax collectors in his home. The "religious authorities" rebuked Jesus by accusing him of eating and drinking with publicans and sinners. Jesus responded, "Those who are well have no need of a physician, but those who are sick. Go and learn what this means, I desire mercy, not sacrifice" (Matthew 9:12-13).

There's a special place in God's kingdom for those who faithfully respond to God's call to become religious leaders. These pastors, priests, and rabbis are special gifts from God. Even though the Gospel of Matthew is particularly critical of certain Jewish religious leaders, no part of the Gospels should be interpreted as, or used to justify, hatred of Jews or any religious group or institution. Jesus taught love and acceptance, not hate and rejection.

Reflection

I've often wondered if Matthew (Levi) had originally prepared for the priesthood and left because of some corruption. This would help explain his frustrations regarding certain religious leaders who neglected their responsibilities. At least tax collectors were open about their shortcomings. Matthew the tax collector would have been barred from the temple and worship life. Matthew may have longed for God's presence in his life. Jesus gave him that second chance.

I'm sure Matthew followed Jesus because he knew he could never find true happiness with worldly possessions. Jesus makes all things new. The transformation of Matthew shows Christ's ability to restore lost relationships with God and with others. A sure sign of Matthew's conversion was his desire to share his newfound joy with other tax collectors.

Levi's name was changed to Matthew, which means, "Gift from God." The name is quite appropriate. Levi had placed his trust in money and was willing to do anything to obtain it. When Jesus called Matthew, it was an act of God's grace. Only God can accept us with such generosity. That's why we call this grace amazing.

There was a nationwide poll a few years ago that asked, "What would you most like to hear?"

The number one response was "I love you."

The second was "You are forgiven."

The third was "Supper is ready."

On the day that changed his life forever, Matthew received all three. God loves, forgives, and calls to supper. Together we gather at the Lord's Table and give God the glory!

Reflection Questions

1. Bishop Theodulf of Spain (750-822) served as a spiritual advisor to Charlemagne, the first great king of Europe. His hymn was based on the Matthew text for Palm Sunday. What does it mean to call Jesus the Lord of Lords and King of Kings?

All glory, laud, and honor, to thee, Redeemer, King,
To whom the lips of children, made sweet hosannas ring.
Thou art the King of Israel, thou David's royal son,
Who in the Lord's name comest, the King and Blessed One.
The company of angels, are praising thee on high,
And mortal men and all things, created make reply.
Thou didst accept their praises: accept the prayers we bring,
Who in all good delightest, thou good and gracious King.

2. When Jesus called Matthew to follow him, Matthew responded immediately. Have you ever felt such a call? If so, describe it.

3. Reflect on God's willingness to forgive and accept us. Do you need to forgive anyone right now?

12

Lydia

Read: Acts 16:11-15

Background

The city of Philippi was named after Alexander the Great's father who conquered it in 355 BC. Local gold mines financed many military campaigns. The city was fortunate because it backed the winning side of Mark Anthony and Octavian (Caesar Augustus) versus Cassius and Brutus in 42 BC. Many considered the battle a moral victory because Brutus and Cassius had assassinated Julius Caesar. They both lost their lives. Many Philippians were rewarded with the great gift of Roman freedom and privilege.

The city was a major seaport located between Greece and Turkey. It was a trading center along the Via Egnatia, the major Roman highway that linked Western Europe with the Persian East. A cosmopolitan city, Philippi blended Greek and Latin traditions. Philippi was the site of the first Christian church in Europe.

Lydia lived in Philippi and was known as a "God fearing" person. This meant she was a Gentile who converted to Judaism. Many people were attracted by Jewish discipline, business success, moral character, love of family, and kindness toward others. She rejected the pagan lifestyle and sought a closer walk with God

Lydia was a successful businesswoman. She sold purple cloth, a very rare commodity. The purple dye was obtained from scraping thousands of small carnivorous shellfish (like crab and lobster). Because of Roman law (and cost), the wearing of purple garments was limited to the privileged classes.

Lydia belonged to a local Jewish congregation that had no building or synagogue. They worshiped weekly on the bank of a local river. One Sabbath, Paul and Silas joined them at worship and shared the good news about Jesus. While Paul was preaching, "the Lord opened her heart" (Acts 16:14). Lydia was a decisive person. This was the salvation she was seeking. She dedicated her life to Christ, and her entire household was baptized with her.

Lydia next demonstrated the confidence and determination of a true entrepreneur and a true host. She urged Paul and companions to stay at her home, which was large enough to accommodate many guests. It later became headquarters for the church in Philippi and Lydia became its leader. Her hospitality was a remarkable gift!

Paul and Silas experienced difficult times in Philippi. They were falsely arrested, beaten, and imprisoned. There was an earthquake, and they used the crisis as an opportunity to witness to their fellow prisoners. They sang hymns of praise. They even witnessed to their jailer. Paul and Silas, entrepreneurs for Christ, never missed an opportunity to evangelize. Eventually they were released and Lydia welcomed them once again into her home.

The church in Philippi became Paul's favorite. Years later, while imprisoned, Paul would receive gifts of support from Philippi (Philippians 4:16). When starvation struck the mother church in Jerusalem, Philippi came to the rescue with great generosity. Paul referred to Philippi as a community of great joy (Philippians 1:3).

Reflections

Lydia knew the rich and famous of her day but found her purpose in life through her relationship with the risen Lord Jesus. Lydia knew a real king when she saw one. Christ was dressed in clothes of compassion, forgiveness, and friendship. Lydia and the church of Philippi shared that message with others.

True friendship is always active, not passive. Jesus asks us to care for those in need. Lydia and the Philippian church repeatedly showed their great generosity.

A friend is candid. God wants us to honestly engage with him. True friends are open with each other. Lydia did not hesitate to speak her mind.

A friend is giving. True friends are willing to share everything. The church in Philippi generously helped others in need.

A friend is loyal. True friends care for each other through good times and bad. The Philippians earned special freedoms because of loyalty to Rome. Now they were devoted to God. Philippi faithfully supported Paul when he was arrested.

A friend can be a source of joy. The book of Philippians is known as the epistle of joy. Like Paul and Silas, we can experience great joy after times of significant struggle. Joy is like the sunrise that follows the darkest hours of our lives.

John Scriven, a Canadian immigrant, understood the meaning of true friendship. During a particularly difficult time in his life, he tragically suffered the loss of loved ones. Rather than submit to anger or depression, he dedicated himself to helping others. He devoted his days (and possessions) to the feeding and caring for widows, orphans, and the poor. He could not afford to visit his ailing mother (back in England) so he wrote her these words:

What a Friend we have in Jesus, all our sins and grief's to bear!
What a privilege to carry everything to God in prayer!
O what peace we often forfeit, O what needless pain we bear,
All because we do not carry everything to God in prayer.
Have we trials and temptations? Is there trouble anywhere?
We should never be discouraged; take it to the Lord in prayer.
Can we find a friend so faithful who will all our sorrows share?
Jesus knows our every weakness; take it to the Lord in prayer.
Are we weak and heavy laden, cumbered with a load of care?
Precious Savior, still our refuge, take it to the Lord in prayer.
Do your friends despise, forsake you? Take it to the Lord in prayer!
In His arms He'll take and shield you; you will find a solace there.
(1855)

Reflection Questions

1. What does it mean to have Jesus as a friend? Is your friendship with Jesus active? How does this impact your other friendships?

2. What person or persons do you know who display their Christian faith in the way they conduct themselves in their work or business?

3. The church in Philippi was known for its generosity and joy. In what ways is your church modeling this kind of generosity? Sharing joy?

13
Stephen

Read: Acts 7:54-60

Background

The apostles were very busy in the early Christian church. Acts 6 describes how they were overworked and needed help. They called seven Greek-speaking followers of Jesus to help with the care and feeding of widows and orphans. The Greek word for "serving others" used in this story is the word from which we get the word *deacon*. They were called "to wait on tables." This is the same type of humble service that Jesus once provided for his disciples. Jesus cleansed the disciples' feet before feeding their bodies and souls.

These servants of Christ were commissioned in a special ceremony that included "laying on of hands." This was the same temple ritual used for the sacrifice of sacred animals. In the Old Testament, lives were taken away. In the New Testament, lives were given away. These servants offered themselves as "living sacrifices" to God.

Stephen is described as being "full of grace and power, he did great wonders and signs among the people" (Acts 6:8). He served food, but he also nourished people's spirits.

Stephen spoke out regularly, telling others about the salvation of our Lord Jesus Christ. His work was so successful that leaders in the temple began to plot against him. With false witnesses they fabricated charges and brought him to trial. They accused Stephen of "sinning against" Moses, the Temple, and the Torah (the first five books of the Hebrew Scriptures). Technically, none of these were really illegal.

Stephen didn't waste time refuting their petty charges. He seized the opportunity to share the world's greatest truth. Stephen's

37

dramatic speech is the longest recorded in the book of Acts. He quoted from the Old Testament twenty-two times explaining God's message is never limited to one person, place, or book. He made several charges of his own:

The religious leaders were "stiff-necked" when they ignored God's special messengers. They were more interested in worshiping "things" like the Temple and Torah. At Mount Sinai, the people rejected Moses and the Commandments by worshiping a golden calf.

Some people in Israel considered themselves saved because of their nationality. God's salvation is not limited to any particular nation. God's saving grace is universal.

Israel had a history of mistreating God's messengers. The people had ignored or persecuted the prophets. Even the sons of Jacob (Israel) sold their brother Joseph into slavery (Genesis 37).

Stephen called his accusers "betrayers and murderers" of "God's Righteous One" (Acts 7:52). He asserted they were the real lawbreakers. The truth hurt. They cried out with a loud voice and angrily rushed upon him. They dragged him from the city of Jerusalem and stoned him (because their laws forbade killing anyone within the city walls).

Stephen knelt down and cried out in a loud voice, "Lord, do not hold this sin against them" (Acts 7:60). Stephen had a forgiving spirit as Jesus did upon the cross. He was transfigured before his accusers. They "saw his face was like that of an angel." In this moment of genuine worship, Stephen saw the glory of God. While they were stoning him, Stephen prayed, "Lord Jesus, receive my spirit," and then he died. In a similar manner, Jesus had said, "It is finished." Then he bowed his head and gave up his spirit (John 19:30).

Reflections

St. Francis of Assisi wrote: "Keep a clear eye toward life's end. Do not forget your purpose and destiny as God's creature. . . . Remember that when you leave this earth, you can take with you nothing that you have received—fading symbols of honor, trappings of power— but only what you have given: a full heart enriched by honest service, love, sacrifice, and courage" (*Letters to Rulers of People*, c.1220).

Stephen, the first martyr, was a church volunteer. Anyone can make a big difference in God's kingdom. Stephen did not have years of training, but he used his gifts to make an important difference in the church. Church tradition states that he was still wearing his serving apron when he died.

Saul of Tarsus was present at the stoning. Coats were laid at his feet. This reveals he was in charge (Acts 7:58). St. Augustine said, "If Stephen had not prayed (and was stoned to death for it), the Church would not have gained Paul." Saul must have been moved by the power of Stephen's faith.

The name *Stephen* is Greek for "crown," the type of special wreath placed on the head of an Olympic winner. Saint Stephen forever wears the great crown of glory in God's kingdom and shares eternally in the victory that Christ won for us all.

Reflection Questions

1. Hymnist Horatio Bolton Nelson, Lord Admiral Nelson's grandnephew, understood conflict and wrestled with the meaning of personal sacrifice. What sacrifices do modern Christians make?

From all Thy saints in warfare, for all Thy saints at rest,
To Thee, O blessed Jesus, all praises be addressed;
Thou, Lord, didst win the battle, that they might conquerors be;
Their crowns of living glory are lit with rays from Thee.

Praise for the first of martyrs, who saw Thee ready stand
To aid in midst of torments, to plead at God's right hand.
Share we with him, if summoned by death our Lord to own,
On earth the faithful witness, in heaven the martyr's crown. (1864)

2. What does it mean to be a servant church? How are you a servant in Christ's name? What sacrifices are you willing to make?

3. Stephen worshiped God with all his body, mind, and soul. How does our worship impact all that we say and do?

14

Simeon and Anna

Read: Luke 2:22-38

Background

In this story of the dedication of Jesus, we hear how two special people beheld the promised savior. Male children were traditionally circumcised after eight days. This marked the child's acceptance into the community of faith (Genesis 17:9-14). This was also the special moment a child was given a name. Giving a child a biblical name was considered an act of special blessing. Such a dedication was a commitment to the care of God's love.

Mary and Joseph named their child "Jesus" (from "Joshua" in Hebrew) meaning "God is our salvation." The angel of the Lord had instructed Mary to name her son Jesus. This name was an act of divine fulfillment. He would be the instrument of God's salvation.

Mary and Joseph were too poor to afford the recommended sacrifice of a lamb. They gave the humble offering of two turtledoves (Leviticus 12:6-8). Jesus, the Lamb of God, would later offer the ultimate sacrifice for all of us.

Simeon was present in the temple. God promised that he would see the Savior of the world before he died. His words were, "Master, now you are dismissing your servant in peace, according to your word; for my eyes have seen your salvation, which you have prepared in the presence of all peoples, a light for revelation to the Gentiles and for glory to your people Israel" (Luke 2:29-32). These words proclaim the spiritual gift that God was giving to the whole world.

Simeon's song of praise has been sung in Christian churches for nearly two thousand years. It is called the *Nunc Dimittis* (Latin for "now depart"). It contains the assurance that this faithful servant of

God had seen the fulfillment of God's promise made long ago to Abraham (Genesis 15:15) and to Jacob (Genesis 46:30).

The prophetess Anna was also present. She served in the proud tradition of female prophets throughout Israel's history—Miriam (Exodus 15:20); Deborah (Judges 4:4); Huldah (2 Kings 22:14); and Isaiah's wife (Isaiah 8:3). Anna reestablished the continuing role of women as prophets in the Christian church (Acts 2:17, Acts 21:9, 1 Corinthians 11:5).

The text indicates Anna was eighty-four years old or had lived as a widow for that amount of years. Either way, she had remained faithful in the temple by worshiping, fasting, and praying. We do not know the exact prophetic words of Anna, but we are told that she saw the Christ child as a liberating figure for all the people of God.

Reflections

The worship center is where God is most often revealed to us, where we often wait with patience to hear God's promises. Simeon sought salvation in the temple. Worship is exercising patience as we wait to hear the Word of God. The best place to worship is in the house of God. Worship is the most important thing we do. The commandments tell us to keep the Sabbath Day holy for good reason. Worship is the time we gather to sing praises and open ourselves to hearing God's Word. Worship keeps our relationship with God in focus.

We worship as a community of believers. Jesus said, "Wherever two or more are gathered [in the context of worship], I am with you" (Matthew 18:20). Jesus stressed the importance of worship throughout his ministry. Jesus began his ministry proclaiming the word of God in a worship center (Luke 4:16-27).

Some Christians maintain they can worship God outside of the church. They sit alone in their homes or "worship" outside amidst the beauty of creation. They miss the opportunity to share worship with the fellowship of all believers. Jesus regularly demonstrated the need to gather with others in worship.

A sad detail of American history is that very few of Patrick Henry's revolutionary speeches were ever written down. He is famous for his rousing statement made in St. James Church in 1775,

"Give me liberty or give me death!" This speech was reconstructed forty years later (over fifteen years after his death). Henry kept few notes and the spellbound audience failed to take notes. Despite our lack of details we know his messages encouraged liberty for all.

Anna's speech must have been just as inspiring. Scripture indicates that Anna spoke of Jesus' great gift of spiritual freedom. Jesus brought us independence from those things that separate us from God. Worship is the place where we share these messages of salvation. Church is where it's happening!

Anna was a prophet (which means to "speak or proclaim" God's word). The name *Anna* means "God's grace." The name *Simeon* means, "to listen." Together in worship they heard the world's greatest messenger: "And the Word became flesh and lived among us, and we have seen his glory, the glory as of a father's only son, full of grace and truth" (John 1:14). This is the greatest story ever told!

Reflection Questions

1. Isaac Watts (1674-1748) sang praises to God throughout his life. He wrote six hundred hymns including "O God Our Help in Ages Past." What does it mean to depart in peace?

Now have our hearts embraced our God, we would forget all earthly charms,

And wish to die, as Simeon would, with his young Savior in his arms.

Our lips should learn that joyful song, were but our hearts prepared like his

Our souls still willing to be gone, and at thy word depart in peace.

2. What kinds of peace does Jesus bring? In what ways does Jesus bring us freedom? How can we share this gift with others?

3. How does God speak to you in worship? What can we learn from Simeon and Anna about persistent patience? How does worship impact your work and everyday life?

15
Nicodemus

Read: John 3:1-21

Background

Nicodemus was a Pharisee who came from a very distinguished family. Historical records indicate members of his family occasionally served as official ambassadors to Rome.

Nicodemus was probably a member of the Sanhedrin, a ruling body that had religious jurisdiction over every Jew in the world. It was their responsibility to deal with anyone suspected of being a false prophet.

Nicodemus came to Jesus at night. Why? Rabbis declared that the best time to study was at night when a person would not be disturbed (Jesus would have been surrounded by crowds during the day). Nicodemus may also have been a very cautious man and not ready to meet with Jesus in public. Nicodemus may have simply been on a fact-finding journey. Whatever the reason, Jesus graciously welcomed him.

Nicodemus immediately treated Jesus with great respect by calling him "rabbi." He was like a new "disciple" with many questions. A sign of great wisdom is realizing how much we don't know and having a willingness to learn more.

Jesus confirmed that he was truly God's messenger. He stated that a person must be "born again" or, better yet, "born from above" in order to be a part of God's kingdom. Here, the Greek word that Jesus used to describe this phrase has three possible meanings:

It can mean a radical change in life, like the birth of a child.

It can mean "again," as in second physical birth.

Finally, it can mean a "spiritual" or "heavenly" birth. This can only be accomplished with God's divine intervention into our lives.

Nicodemus was confused. He understood the phrase in a literal way, a second physical birth. But he realized it was impossible to reenter the womb!

Jesus' response reveals that this change in our lives happens through the power of God's Spirit. In baptism, we are reborn by this Spirit. We can never accomplish any real change on our own; this change is a gift of God's love and grace.

Nicodemus' final question indicated he was still in the dark. Jesus' response could be translated as, "Hey, you're supposed to be the teacher, and yet I'm the one teaching you!"

Jesus responds with what Martin Luther called "the Gospel in miniature": "For God so loved the world that he gave his only Son, so that everyone who believes in him may not perish but may have eternal life" (John 3:16).

We see a spiritual journey unfold in Nicodemus' life. He began his journey "at night" with the first hesitant steps to find answers. Later he cautiously defended Jesus before the Sanhedrin saying, "Does our law not judge people without first giving them a hearing?" (John 7:51). Finally, Nicodemus joined Joseph from Arimathea to care for the body of Jesus after the crucifixion (John 19:39-42). Early church tradition maintains that Nicodemus continued to grow in his faith and remained a faithful follower of Christ.

Reflections

God sent Jesus into the world so that we can have new life from faith. "Everlasting life" is just not the promise of fellowship with God in the hereafter. It is also an abundant and meaningful life we can immediately realize. This salvation can happen now!

The early church refers to baptism as a "sacrament," from a Latin word meaning "gift from God." Baptism is a new birth. Paul spoke of a person dying with Christ and then rising to a new life (Romans 6:1-11). In baptism we drown to worldly ways and then God's Spirit breathes new life into us. We are born from above. Paul speaks of new converts as babies in Christ (1 Corinthians 3:1-2). In Christ we are a new creation (Galatians 6:15).

Baptism is God's **cleansing**. We realize that we are not saved by our own efforts. We humbly recognize that we need God to wash away our sin (1 Peter 3:21-22; Acts 22:16). This is like the story of Noah's ark. The waters cleansed the earth but the faithful were saved from chaos and death (1 Peter 3:18-22).

We are baptized into the **family** of God. We are adopted into the fellowship of believers (Ephesians 1:3-5; Galatians 3:25-29). We belong to God's family (2 Corinthians 5:17). This relationship is sealed by the power of the Holy Spirit (Ephesians 1:13-14; 2 Corinthians 1:21-22).

Baptism is best described as a way of life. This is not just a one-time event, but also a great gift that must be celebrated and appreciated every day of our lives. Living in our baptism we find a new purpose for all that we do (Ephesians 5:14).

The name *Nicodemus* means "victor over the people." Nicodemus was certainly an influential person when he came to visit Jesus. That night he began a spiritual journey. Nicodemus graciously helped minister to the crucified Christ. On Easter Sunday he discovered that Jesus was the real victor. By his death Jesus defeated the power of death. Christ is the ultimate victor!

Reflection Questions

1. Susan Helen Peterson dedicated her life to sharing Christ's salvation with others. Her final hymn speaks of being "born anew." What does this mean to you?

A man named Nicodemus to Jesus came one night.
He said, "We know you've come from God; your wonders show his
    might."
In answer, Jesus did declare, "Give heed, these words are true:
You cannot see God's kingdom come unless you're born anew."
(1999)

2. What does your baptism mean to you? Describe a "baptismal way of life."

3. In what ways can you be available to those seeking answers? Do you place limits on your availability? What people have helped you most in your "walk of faith"?

<u>16</u>

John

Read: Luke 9:51-56

Background

John was a son of Zebedee, a fishing boat owner on the Sea of Galilee. John and his older brother James were called to follow Jesus to become fishers of men. They obeyed and followed.

In the beginning, John was quite an aggressive person. He and James received the nicknames "sons of thunder" for their quixotic tempers. There was the incident when a Samaritan town refused passage for Jesus and his followers. James and John were prepared to blast the village out of existence. Jesus, the Prince of Peace, quieted things down, and they proceeded on their journey with no violence to the village.

One day, James and John inappropriately asked if they could have a special place of honor when Jesus came into his kingdom. The other disciples were upset with this attempt to gain power and favoritism. Jesus in turn taught that those who would be first in God's kingdom must first be humble servants of all (Mark 10:35; Matthew 20:20).

John eventually experienced a transformation while following Jesus. This angry and ambitious man became a devoted disciple. Such is the power of Christ to change lives. John was the only disciple who followed Jesus to Golgotha. From the cross, Jesus asked John to care for Mary, his mother. Jesus must have had great love for them both. John came to be known as "the beloved disciple."

Reflections

The Guinness Book of World Records lists the shortest sermon ever preached. John Albrecht, an Episcopal priest in Michigan, gave it. He stood in his pulpit to preach, paused, and said "Love!" He then sat down. Some said it was the best sermon ever preached.

One can imagine John as a beloved leader of the early church teaching a congregation about Jesus. They could see the transformation for themselves. Jerome (an early church Biblical scholar) tells the story of John's last words. When John was dying, his disciples asked him if he had any last message for them. "Little children," he said, "you should love one another." He repeated it again and again, and they asked him if there was anything else. "Love is enough," John said, "for it is the Lord's greatest command."

John had discovered what matters most in life. Life is all about God's love. God wants the fellowship of believers to be known for love. Jesus said our love for each other is our greatest witness to the world. "My children, I will be with you for a little while longer. Then you will look for me, but you won't find me. I tell you just as I told the people, you cannot go where I am going. But I am giving you a new command. You must love each other, just as I have loved you. If you love each other, everyone will know that you are my disciples" (John 13:33-35).

Early tradition indicates that John moved to Ephesus and became the bishop of Asia Minor (modern day Turkey). Tradition also indicates he was banished to the prison island of Patmos for many years. Some claim Mary, mother of Jesus, accompanied him and she became a valued partner in ministry. It would be great to have a time machine to go back and personally observe these many details.

The presence of John and Mary in Ephesus would have been a great irony. Ephesus was known as "the gateway to Asia." It was a major crossroads for those traveling to Rome. The word *Ephesus* means "appetite." Many worldly hungers were satisfied there.

Ephesus was the site of the temple of Artemis, the goddess of fertility and love. This temple was considered one of the seven great wonders of the ancient world. It was also the banking and commercial center of the city. Within the temple, young women were forced into sexual slavery. The pagan leaders believed these physical acts of "love" guaranteed good harvests and financial prosperity. This was not love; it was an ungodly act of violence.

John and Mary stood for a different type of love, a sacrificial love, God's love. Saint Paul described this love in a letter to a sister church: "Love is patient; love is kind; love is not envious or boastful or arrogant or rude. It does not insist on its own way; it is not irritable or resentful; it does not rejoice in wrongdoing, but rejoices in the truth. It bears all things, believes all things, hopes all things, and endures all things" (1 Corinthians 13:4-7). This is a heavenly type of love.

John and Mary must have had great success. Traditions indicate that the violent priests of Artemis were so upset that they poisoned John. He survived to lead others to Christ and proclaim a message of God's true love.

Reflection Questions

1. Martin Luther called Bernard of Clairvaux (1091-1153) "the best monk who ever lived." Bernard fought against hatred and anti-Semitism. He based this hymn of love on the first chapter of John. How do these verses reflect John's message? How is life new?

O Jesus, joy of loving hearts, the fount of life, the light of all:
From every bliss, that earth imparts, we turn, unfilled, to hear your call.
Your truth unchanged, has ever stood; you plead with all to call on you;
To those who seek you, you are good; to those who find you, life is new.

2. Describe "heavenly" love. When and where have you encountered it? How have you shared it?

3. How can we be "beloved disciples" of Christ? In what manner can we follow Christ to the cross today?

17

Cleopas and Companion

Read: Luke 24:13-25

Background

This story shows that Jesus has a divine sense of humor! The narrative describes the glorious day of the resurrection. Jesus had shared the good news with the women and then the disciples. Later, Jesus took a journey with two lesser-known disciples. He walked with them, and because their hearts were heavy and occupied with the recent events regarding Jesus, they never recognized him. They did not realize they were talking with the Risen Lord!

Cleopas and the other unnamed disciple had left town before the good news was announced. These disciples had seen what they believed to be the end of Jesus' remarkable ministry. Though they were not part of the very closest circle of Jesus' disciples, they likely had known Jesus and heard him teach or work miracles. Jesus reached out to the two wanderers, asking why they were so sad. They were amazed at his question! They asked if he was the only person from Jerusalem who did not know what had been happening. Of course, Jesus knew it all.

It's human nature to think we have all the answers. The disciples on the road to Emmaus were missing the most important part of the Easter story. They could have learned the truth from Jesus but they weren't paying attention. They talked more than they listened. They weren't seeing with the eyes of faith.

The party reached Emmaus, and Jesus indicated he was traveling further. The couple asked him to stay and be their guest, so Jesus accepted the invitation. In a moment of divine irony, the guest became the host. Jesus took the bread, blessed it, broke it, and gave it to them. In that moment they realized who he was, and then he was gone.

Jesus used the very same words and actions when he fed the five thousand (Luke 9:16) and presided at the Last Supper (Luke 22:19). These four verbs *(take, bless, break, give)* are Jesus' holy signature. In these moments, the disciples were spiritually fed and their eyes were opened. Being so moved by the revelation of the Risen Lord, they immediately set out for Jerusalem.

Reflection

An unusual study points out that there are plenty of good reasons to attend church:

20 percent of all fatal accidents happen in auto crashes.

17 percent of all fatal accidents occur in the home.

16 percent of all fatal accidents involve some form of public transport (planes, trains, and boats).

14 percent of all fatal accidents involve pedestrians on streets and sidewalks.

Only .001 percent of all fatal accidents occur in worship at church. Logically the safest place at any time is at church!

The first sign of a spiritual setback can be separation from the community of believers. Cleopas and companion chose not to remain in Jerusalem with the other disciples. They handled their loss by leaving town.

Contemporary biblical author Frederick Buechner asserts that Emmaus is a type of place that people go to escape (such as a shopping center, movie, nightclub, cave) when they are frustrated and cannot find answers they are seeking. Emmaus is the way of seeking worldly answers. Emmaus may promise us momentary relief, but can never give us lasting joy.

The disciples who stayed in Jerusalem offered comfort to one another. Fellowships of believers read Scriptures together, share cares and concerns, break bread, and know that Christ is present. The Emmaus disciples finally realized their mistake of leaving their faith community. They hurried back.

Christians are called into community. We are commanded to love each other, pray for each other, encourage each other, admonish each other, greet each other, serve each other, teach each other, accept each other, honor each other, bear each other's burdens, forgive each other, submit to each other, and be devoted to each other.

God's presence is never meant to be a private gift. The experience should be shared. The church is a gift from Christ. Together:

Jesus "takes" us to a fellowship of all believers;
Jesus "blesses" us with a message of love;
Jesus' message "breaks" down things that would divide us; and
Jesus "gives" us back to the world to share his message of salvation.

Jesus assures us that "For where two or three are gathered (in worship) in my name, I am there among them" (Matthew 18:20). The community of believers is forever the place to stay. It's where we belong.

Reflection Questions

1. The Rev. Dr. John Fawcett served the same Baptist church for many years. He wrote this hymn after being tempted to move elsewhere. He stayed. His hymn speaks of burdens to bear. How can we help each other? What does it mean to be the family of God?

Blest be the tie that binds our hearts in Christian love;
the fellowship of kindred minds is like to that above.
Before our Father's throne we pour our ardent prayers;
our fears, our hopes, our aims are one, our comforts and our cares.
We share each other's woes, our mutual burdens bear;
and often for each other flows the sympathizing tear. (1782)

2. Why is it difficult to listen when we are grieving or angry?

3. How can your church better enable you to love, pray, encourage, admonish, greet, serve, teach, accept, honor, and forgive each other? Bear each other's burdens? Submit to each other? Be devoted to each other?

18

Barnabas

Read: Acts 4:32-37

Background

Joseph was someone who made things happen. He was a Levite (priestly family) from the island of Cyprus. He was probably among the pilgrims who heard about Jesus' resurrection and traveled to Jerusalem for the Pentecost celebration, the Jewish harvest festival that took place fifty days after Passover. Peter had given an inspirational sermon, which led to the report that "those who welcomed his message were baptized, and that day about three thousand persons were added. They devoted themselves to the apostles' teaching and fellowship, to the breaking of bread and the prayers" (Acts 2:41-42).

This new fellowship of Jesus' followers cared for each other. No one was in need of anything. Jesus had converted hearts, minds, and pocketbooks. Joseph was an influential landowner. He saw a need and generously donated a piece of property for the work of the church (Acts 4).

The apostles gave Joseph a new name, *Barnabas*, which means "one who shares encouragement." This was an event of great significance. The new name was a sign of his transformation but also revealed he helped others in their ministries.

Barnabas was a respected church leader by the time Saul of Tarsus was persecuting Christians. Saul experienced a radical transformation (Acts 9) and turned his life over to Christ. Saul later changed his name to Paul. Many Christians were still suspicious and considered him a spy. They avoided Paul, but Barnabas gave him a second chance. He introduced Paul to the other disciples. Paul was welcomed because of Barnabas' intervention.

Years later there was great growth in the church of Antioch (third largest city in the Roman empire). The news reached

Jerusalem, and the church leaders sent Barnabas to support the new mission. Barnabas was delighted with the progress but realized he needed help. He sent for Paul. "For an entire year they met with the church and taught a great many people" (Acts 11:26). This was the first place believers were called "Christians."

The young church of Antioch generously sent financial help to Jerusalem during a time of great need. They then decided to send missionaries to reach other people. They commissioned Barnabas, his nephew John Mark, and Paul to start this new ministry. They left for the island of Cyprus and then headed toward the cities of Galatia (the interior of modern day Turkey). Along the way, John Mark abandoned them and returned to Jerusalem (Acts 13).

Paul and Barnabas continued on to Lystra. There they preached in the marketplace, and Paul healed a person who was crippled. The crowd declared them to be "gods" and compared Barnabas to Zeus (a powerful, good-looking Greek god) and Paul to Mercury (the messenger of the gods). Paul and Barnabas used the opportunity to preach about the one true "God." Following this successful mission they returned to Jerusalem (Acts 14).

Some leaders in Jerusalem were concerned about the sudden growth of these new churches. They did not like all the new changes. The "Council of Jerusalem" (Acts 15) was held to determine guidelines for outreach. Many were concerned that the new Gentile followers were not practicing some of the Jewish customs and practices. Paul argued that following certain laws did not have to be a prerequisite for being included in God's new family.

Peter boldly spoke on behalf of sharing Christ's message with all peoples. Jesus' last words had been the Great Commission to "Go therefore and make disciples of all nations, baptizing them in the name of the Father and of the Son and of the Holy Spirit, and teaching them to obey everything that I have commanded you" (Matthew 28:19-20). Some compromises and agreements were made. Worldwide missions were approved. Paul and Barnabas prepared to begin a new journey.

True to form, Barnabas wanted to give John Mark a second chance. Paul did not. The two disagreed and went their separate ways. Paul set off for Asia Minor, Macedonia, and Greece. Barnabas and John Mark returned to the Island of Cyprus. Paul later mentioned a restored relationship with Barnabas and John Mark in his letters. Barnabas, the encourager, eventually taught Paul the lesson of acceptance and giving people a second chance.

Reflections

Barnabas' ministry was always about building up the body of Christ. He's the model of a church leader who can graciously forgive and forget. Barnabas shared the love of Jesus Christ. He talked the talk and walked the walk.

Sometimes a simple word or deed can make all the difference in another person's life. Barnabas helped make possible the ministries of one of the great leaders of the church—Paul, the great evangelist to the Gentiles. His gift of encouragement strengthened the early church in Jerusalem and the churches of Antioch, Cyprus, and Galatia.

When he was called to go and share the gospel, he went. And he supported his partner Paul in the process. Barnabas helps us to reflect on the great purposes God may be calling us to do. In what ways can you help build up the body of Christ, the church? It may not be as dramatic as becoming a traveling missionary, but be certain, there is something for you to do. At the very least, you can live out the meaning of Barnabas' name and be an encourager of others.

Reflection Questions

1. Canterbury Cathedral Dean Henry Alford was known as a caring friend (author of "Come You Thankful People Come"). These verses reflect his appreciation of Barnabas' ministry. What are the gifts of mighty words and wisdom true?

From the Twelve, with love unblamed, "Son of consolation," named.
Blessed Spirit, Who didst call, Barnabas and holy Paul,
And didst them with gifts endue. Mighty words and wisdom true,
Grant us, Lord of life, to be. By their pattern full of Thee. (1844)

2. Which people have encouraged you in your faith journey? What difference has it made?

3. Many ministries could benefit from a "Barnabas Gift." Do you have a possession that could make a significant difference for others? How can we give from our hearts?

19

Mary, John Mark's Mother

Read: Acts 12:6-19

Background

This Mary is mentioned only once in Scripture. Peter was arrested and imprisoned by Herod Agrippa and was awaiting trial and probable execution in Jerusalem. Members of the early church gathered in prayer for his release. An angel interceded and Peter was released from captivity. Later that night, Peter headed for Mary's house to inform others of his escape.

A young servant named Rhoda answered the door. She was so surprised that she left the poor guy standing outside while she ran to tell the others. First, Peter was locked up and then he was locked out! The disciples inside didn't believe Rhoda. Despite their prayers, they could not imagine this miracle had truly happened. Peter kept knocking at the door until they finally let him in (not exactly hospitality at its best!).

Mary's house was large enough to accommodate a large gathering of Christians for prayer and worship. She would have been a woman of some wealth to afford such a large home and maintain a domestic servant. She may have been a widow, but her husband's name is never mentioned.

We do know that Mary was the mother of John Mark, who some believe may have written the Gospel of Mark. John Mark was just a young man while Jesus ministered in Jerusalem. Mark probably grew up hearing the teachings of Jesus and watching the activities of the early church. Mary's close relative, Barnabas, would later take John Mark on a missionary journey with Paul. Mary provided the early church with a place to meet and they in turn helped her son mature into a champion of the faith.

Mixed traditions indicate that Mary's house may have been "The Cenacle" or center of many activities in the early church. They suggest that her home was the location of the upper room where Jesus gathered with his disciples to share the Last Supper. They identify her home as the place the disciples gathered on Easter morning, the site of the great Pentecost event, and many other gatherings of the early church. We simply do not know if all these connections are accurate.

We do know that Mary modeled Christian hospitality in the early church. Jesus relied on hospitality throughout his life and ministry. It began with the innkeeper who provided the manger in a rustic shelter. It included those who supplied food and shelter during his journeys, the home of Mary and Martha, a banquet at Matthew's home, the room for the Last Supper. Even the tomb in which his body was laid was lent to him for his brief stay!

Reflections

The early Christians would gather in homes for fellowship, worship, and discipleship. "They devoted themselves to the apostles' teaching and fellowship, to the breaking of bread and the prayers" (Acts 2:42).

These Christians would share food with each other in what was called an "Agape meal." Agape is a unique word that means "God's love." Agape is the type of love that is inspired and enabled by God. Agape means the hand of God reaches down and gives us a heavenly assist. God's love raises us up to share a special fellowship beyond our human limitations.

The early Christians demonstrated this type of love when they gathered together. Many new converts were attracted to the church because of the genuine care and compassion they witnessed. These Christians modeled their lives by the example set by Jesus. In his book, *The Purpose-Driven Life*, Rick Warren describes ten characteristics of biblical fellowship:

1. Sharing our true feelings (**authenticity**). Romans 12:9
2. Encouraging each other (**mutuality**). Galatians 5:22-26
3. Supporting each other (**sympathy**). Galatians 6:1-2
4. Forgiving each other (**mercy**). Ephesians 4:31-32

5. Speaking truth in love (**honesty**). Ephesians 4:15
6. Admitting our weaknesses (**humility**). Romans 12:16
7. Respecting our differences (**courtesy**). Romans 12:10
8. Allowing no gossiping (**confidentiality**). Ephesians 4:31-32
9. Making the group a priority (**frequency**). Colossians 3:16-17
10. Sharing God's good news with each other (**faith**). Ephesians 5:19-20 (see *The Purpose-Driven Life,* pp. 139-151)

Mary was a gentlewoman. "Gentlemen" and "Gentlewomen" are old English words, which originally meant those who practiced Christian hospitality. A gentleperson is an individual who considers other people's needs first. Gentle people openly shared the love of Christ.

Later the word deteriorated to mean those who had fame, fortune, or possessions. The world is filled with people who pride themselves on their independence and self-sufficiency while ignoring the needs of others. Christians are called to rise above self-centered concerns. Christ taught that the most important things in life are shared with others. We only need the love of Christ in our hearts to be God's gentleperson.

Mary's gentility enabled the struggling early church to have a special place for fellowship. I like to think that Mary's home had a plaque at the front door which read "As for me and my household, we will serve the LORD" (Joshua 24:15).

Reflection Questions

1. Father Frederick Faber began many communities of faith to help the lost and poor. He once converted a tavern into a place of holy sanctuary. How do his verses describe God's love?

There's a wideness in God's mercy, like the wideness of the sea;
There's a kindness in His justice, which is more than liberty.
There is welcome for the sinner, and more graces for the good;
There is mercy with the Savior; there is healing in His blood.
There is grace enough for thousands, of new worlds as great as this;
There is room for fresh creations, in that upper home of bliss. (1854)

2. In which ways do you (or your church) demonstrate biblical fellowship? Authenticity? Mutuality? Sympathy? Mercy? Honesty? Humility? Courtesy? Confidentiality? Frequency? Faith?

3. In what ways are you a "gentleperson"?

20

The Prodigal Son, the Waiting Father, and the Jealous Brother

Read: Luke 15:11-32

Background

This has been called the best short story in the world. Shakespeare referred to it more than any other parable. Commentators maintain it is at the heart of Luke's Gospel and perhaps the entire New Testament. The phrase "the Prodigal Son" is not found anywhere in the Bible. That name discounts the equally important roles of the loving father and the older brother.

The story itself is really quite outrageous. It may be difficult to imagine everyday life for a Middle Eastern family two thousand years ago, but this sort of thing just never happened. Jesus' audience knew it too. First, there's the son who prematurely asked his father for his share of the inheritance. Such a request was like saying, "Gee Dad, I wish you were dead!" The son wanted to live the good life, immediately.

Amazingly the father granted the request. No father could be that good. He was willing to allow his precious child to have complete freedom of choice. What love this parent must have had. Most parents would refuse such a request or argue with the wayward child. Not here.

Jesus' audience was hooked. The plot was so shocking that they couldn't wait to hear what happened next. Besides, the story addressed issues that every parent identifies with: what to do with a troublesome child?

The son took off for distant lands (a foreign country). He squandered the money with loose living. Famine struck the land and the son was starving. The only job he could find was tending pigs (a great offense for any respectable Jew). The young man's humiliation was complete. Jesus' listeners probably felt he got what he deserved.

In that moment of crisis, the son repented. The word *repents* means to "turn the other way." He "came to himself" and acknowledged that he'd sinned against both God and his father. He did not deserve to be called his father's son. A plan of salvation began to form. He'd return home and offer to be his father's servant. Even a humble servant in his father's home was better off than he was.

The story then centers on the father. No image comes closer to the true character of God than that of the waiting father. This parent was waiting for the son to return. When he saw the son, he unabashedly ran out to greet him. Outrageous behavior! No reasonable, self-respecting parent would forgive the child nor disgrace himself by running in public. It just wasn't done. It was a loss of dignity. It was humiliating! But God's grace defies human logic because it is astounding and abundant! The foolishness of God exceeds our wisdom.

The father embraced the son before anyone could turn him away. The father did not wait for any apology or explanation. The father accepted the son simply because he showed up. This was agape love. This was heavenly love. The son was welcomed and the celebration began.

The older son also showed up. There are many biblical stories of brothers in conflict (Cain and Abel, Jacob and Esau, Joseph and his brothers). The older brother was outraged! He insulted his father by refusing to join the celebration. The anger was obvious as this son made unproven accusations against his brother involving prostitutes. There was hatred in his heart. The father's heart was broken. This son rejected the greatest inheritance of all: a father's love. The story is left open-ended. We never find out if the entire family was ever fully reconciled.

Reflections

Jesus is reminding us that we are all given the ministry of restoring relationships. The older brother had difficulty overlooking what he felt was his father's favored treatment of his reckless little brother.

He struggled with his father's easy forgiveness. In his anger he isolated himself from the world's most loving parent.

God calls us into relationships of reconciliation. The Lord's Prayer states, "forgive us our sins as we forgive those who sin against us." One is not possible without the other. We are just as guilty as the older brother if we cannot forgive. Through the ages, this parable speaks to us all on many levels: teenage rebellion, inheritance, alienation from family, the appeal of the different, the true cost of foolish living, self-awakening, repentance, homecoming, forgiveness, celebration, sibling rivalry, anger, and broken hearts.

A better title for this parable could be "The Loving Father." Ultimately, that's what counts. God created us to be like the parent. Our purpose is to embrace God's acceptance and share it with others. It's a love that's certainly shocking. Isn't that marvelous?

Reflection Questions

1. Baptist minister Robert Lowry composed hymns of hope in the midst of great personal struggle (he also wrote "Shall We Gather at the River"). What do these verses say about the love of God?

Where is my wandering boy tonight—The boy of my tenderest care,
The boy that was once my joy and light, the child of my love and
*   prayer?*
Go for my wandering boy tonight; Go search for him where you will;
But bring him to me with all his blight, and tell him I love him still.
(1877)

2. With what character do you most closely identify in this parable? Why?

3. The parable may have been told specifically to those who want to set limits on God's love and forgiveness, or who want the church to be only for the "right kind" of people. What are your thoughts about this?

21

Simon the Pharisee

Read: Luke 7:36-50

Background

One day a religious leader named Simon invited Jesus to dinner. It's obvious from the story that Simon was not a very gracious host.

Simon may have invited Jesus into his home to obtain information to use against him.

Simon may have been a showoff who liked to mingle with the famous.

Simon may have seen Jesus as a passing fad and wanted to take advantage of his fifteen minutes of fame.

When guests entered a home there were three things that were traditionally done:

The host would place his hands on the guest's shoulders and *share the kiss of peace.* This was a sign of respect. This ancient practice is the origin of the European custom of kissing friends on the cheeks. Many churches echo this practice by shaking hands while sharing the peace (2 Samuel 15:5; Luke 15:20; Luke 22:47-48).

They would *wash the guest's feet.* Roads were not paved and feet were filthy. Guests ate reclined in close proximity to the food. Cleaning the feet was not only comforting but a sanitary practice (Gen 18:4; 19:2; Judges 19:21; 1 Sam 25:41; John 13:3-5).

They would *put sweet-smelling perfume on the guest's head.* The floral aroma would counter the odors of the outside world. It was the host's responsibility to make sure that the dining experience was pleasant for everyone (Psalms 23:5; Psalm 133:2; Mark 14:3).

Simon did none of these things. He received Jesus into his home and treated him in a contemptible manner. During the meal a woman came in and poured ointment on Jesus' head. This was an extremely generous gift. The perfumed oil was very expensive, and she cared for Jesus in a manner befitting an honored guest.

She humbled herself by washing Jesus' feet with her tears. She dried them with her hair. This woman's actions exhibited love and gratitude. Her actions were the opposite of Simon's. Both violated accepted social customs. One cared beyond expectation, and the other didn't care at all. The woman's actions were as spontaneous as Simon's were cold and calculating.

In this story, we gain a glimpse of Simon's soul. Simon assumed the woman was a sinner. Further, Simon asserted that Jesus was no prophet because he would have known what type of person she was and avoided her.

It was common practice for guests at banquets to share contests of wit and wisdom. The host provided food for the body, and the guest would provide nourishment for the mind. Jesus told a clever story of two men with unpayable debts. One owed much and the other owed little. Both obligations were magnanimously cancelled. Jesus asked, "Which man was more thankful?"

Simon responded, "The man with the greater debt forgiven was more thankful." Jesus confirmed that Simon had given the right answer and then compared the story to the woman's act of love and gratitude. Jesus criticized Simon for his inhospitality and declared that the woman's sins were forgiven.

Reflections

Jesus said, "Not everyone who says to me, 'Lord, Lord,' will enter the kingdom of heaven, but only those who do the will of my Father in heaven" (Matthew 7:21). Simon knew Jesus, invited him into his home, and yet never listened to his message.

Simon considered himself religiously pure, while he considered the woman to be unclean. Simon thought his actions made him righteous before God. He was earning salvation through his own merits. Such people see others as being in need of a savior, but they miss the fact that they themselves also need forgiveness. Self-right-eous behavior can destroy churches and drive spiritual seekers away. Jesus exemplified a different way. He sought out those who were considered unclean or outcast. He showed us how we are called to love and care for all God's children.

Jesus concluded his riddle at the meal with a thought-provoking question. Did the woman love God because she had been forgiven, or was she forgiven because of her love? The woman's sins are never identified. It would be inappropriate to accept Simon's accusations as fact. Jesus did not care and neither should we.

Those who know Jesus naturally do his will. Jesus is all about forgiveness and helping us keep a right relationship with God. We can never earn salvation on our own. We humbly welcome Christ's forgiveness into our lives, and then as good hosts, share it generously with others. "Come Lord Jesus, be our guest and let your gifts to us be blessed. Amen."

Reflection Questions

1. Fanny Crosby, blind author of eight thousand hymns, including *Blessed Assurance*, was dedicated to helping the poor and lost. How can we be more like Jesus? How can we serve Jesus?

Oh, to be nearer, nearer, the feet of my Lord and King!
Oh, to enjoy His presence, and only His love to sing!
Oh, for a faith still brighter, and clearer from day to day!
Oh, to be more like Jesus, in all that I do and say! (1881)

2. How can we show respect for visitors at our church and in our homes?

3. Why are Christians so critical of others at times? How can we work toward unity?

22

The Blind Man

Read: John 9:1-41

Background

John had fun with this story. Gentiles were an important part of his audience, so he wrote this story in the style of popular Greek drama. There are seven scenes, and each scene has only two groups of people speaking. The scenes are arranged in the ancient literary pattern called a *chiasm*. Here's the pattern:

Scene 1—Focuses on **SIN**. Did it cause the man's blindness?
 Scene 2—Focuses on **JESUS** as a healer.
  Scene 3—Focuses on the **PHARISEES** who hinder Jesus' work.
   Scene 4—Focuses on the man's **PARENTS** and their response.
  Scene 5—Focuses on the **PHARISEES** who reject Jesus' miracle.
 Scene 6—Focuses on **JESUS** as savior.
Scene 7—Focuses on **SIN**. The Pharisees remain in sin; they refuse to "see" with the eyes of faith.

The story opens with the disciples asking about the man's blindness. Popular belief assumed that some sinful action by the man or his parents caused the blindness. Jesus disagreed, saying neither was the case. And though the man had been physically blind, his faith allowed him to see Jesus for who he really was, the Son of Man and the Messiah. The Pharisees could physically see, but they were spiritually blind. They could not see Jesus for who he really was. They wanted to argue a point of God's law, while Jesus simply wanted to act out God's love in their midst.

Scene 1 (John 9:1-7) God can use a crisis or conflict to help us grow. We all experience loss in our lives. The most difficult times in our lives can be moments for great witness and growth. These are like spiritual growing pains. Jesus heals the man.

Scene 2 (John 9:8-12) The neighbors question the blind man and find out that Jesus is responsible for the healing. These neighbors do nothing and miss their opportunity to encounter Jesus themselves.

Scene 3 (John 9:13-18) The man visits the temple. A religious trial begins. The religious leaders compel the man to make his first statement of faith. He declares that Jesus is a prophet, a messenger of God. He's begun his faith journey.

Scene 4 (John 9:19-23) The parents are afraid to speak out. They are afraid to make a public witness of their convictions. The path of faith can lead to challenge and conflict. The parents do not defend their own child. Their actions appear to be a form of spiritual cowardice.

Scene 5 (John 9:24-34) The faith fight comes into focus. The healed man mocks the religious leaders. He realizes they are the real sinners. Their spiritual blindness is contrary to the will of God. They cast him out of the worship center.

Scene 6 (John 9:35-38) The man's faith journey enables him to publicly confess Jesus as the Messiah (Savior). Spiritual healing happens when we make public "statements of faith."

Scene 7 (John 9:39-41) The final scene. A severe judgment is pronounced on the religious leaders. They are spiritually blind. Only the faithful have vision.

Reflections

Helen Keller once said, "The saddest thing in the world are people who can see but have no vision." Jesus helps us understand God's vision and purposes for our lives. Jesus points out that the greatest sin is not immoral behavior but ignoring God's will.

The blind man goes through a time of crisis but then begins a journey of spiritual discovery. He is literally brought out of the darkness into the light. Jesus shows the way.

We all experience times of crisis in our lives. We realize we are vulnerable. We realize we need God's help. We realize how incomplete we are without God. We need to make a statement of faith (like the blind man's) to follow Jesus. We need to have courage. True disciples accept God's transforming power and then share it with others.

There are early church paintings in the Roman catacombs linking baptism with this story of the blind man. Both are important symbols of faith and new life. Both enable lives to have new meaning and direction. Both are times of great change.

The writer of the Gospel of John used a popular dramatic form to tell the story of the blind man and Jesus. Those who knew this form would likely have been able to "see" better what he was trying to say. We too must be willing to share the message anew for our contemporary audience. Think of the many ways—modern music, drama, and media to name a few—we can tell that old, old story.

Reflection Questions

1. John Newton, a slave captain, was transformed and became an abolitionist minister. How was he blind and lost? What difference does grace make? Why is it precious?

Amazing grace! How sweet the sound, that saved a wretch like me!
I once was lost, but now am found, was blind, but now I see.
'Twas grace that taught my heart to fear, and grace my fears relieved;
How precious did that grace appear, the hour I first believed.
Through many dangers, toils and snares, I have already come;
'Tis grace hath brought me safe thus far, and grace will lead me
     home. (1779)

2. God often uses people, circumstances, or God's word to change our lives. How have you experienced change in your life?

3. How has the Holy Spirit transformed your way of seeing things?

23

The Woman at the Well

Read: John 4:4-30

Background

This story begins with Jesus and his followers traveling through the rugged back hills of Samaria. Jesus was likely tired and thirsty. He sent the disciples into town to gather food while he sat by a well. A woman came to gather water. It was high noon, the brightest and hottest time of the day. Jesus politely asked her for some water. She was shocked that a Jewish religious leader would ask a Samaritan woman for anything. She teased Jesus for not having a bucket and rope. Because the well was quite deep, no one could get water from it without the right tools.

Jesus responded that he had something much greater to offer her. Jesus could nourish her life with everlasting spiritual waters. He had found a way to effectively engage the woman in conversation. Intrigued, she gave him a drink. Her act of charity led to a life-changing event as she moved from servanthood to discipleship.

The woman realized that Jesus was a gifted messenger from God. Jesus spoke of her life struggles. She'd had five husbands, and she was currently living with a man who was not her husband. She may have been a social outcast. Women usually gathered water in the cool of the morning or at twilight. She may have come at noon to hide her embarrassment. She was amazed at Christ's ability to understand her situation and yet show compassion.

Jesus did not condemn or attempt to shame her. This was never his agenda. They spoke of the importance of worship locations. He told the woman that God is more interested in spiritual matters than mundane material ones. Jesus assured the woman that the Samaritans were very important to God. All people are.

Jesus dipped deep into her life and gave her spiritual refreshment. The woman welcomed this gift of grace and immediately shared it with others. She became an evangelist. In her excitement, she forgot her bucket and ran into town proclaiming the arrival of the Savior. Courageously she told everyone "he knows me" and yet, "he accepts me!" "Can he be the Savior?" "Come and see for yourselves!" The townspeople came. Many accepted Jesus as their Lord. The woman had become a "well" filled with God's grace.

Reflections

There is an ancient story of a pilgrim who found a precious gemstone. He put it in his pocket and continued on his journey. One day a fellow traveler was hungry and asked him for food. The pilgrim had none, but he generously gave him the gem so that he might obtain provisions.

The fellow traveler was overjoyed at his good fortune but quickly returned the gift. "Please," he begged, "share with me that which prompted you to share your gift with me."

The story of the Samaritan woman demonstrates that God equips us all to be evangelists. When God accepts us, we have a story to tell. We become wellsprings of God's grace. We are all called to bear witness to this life-changing experience. Jesus treated the woman as a partner in mission. So are we!

This entire story was an adventure of new discovery for the Samaritan woman *(and us)*:

She thought Jesus wanted something from her. She came to realize that he offered her the world's greatest treasure. *(God gives us so much and asks so little in return.)*

She assumed Jacob was greater than Jesus, not realizing Jesus was the savior of all. *(Sometimes we cling to established traditions over listening anew to God.)*

She came to the well to get a simple drink of water and left with a spring of life eternal. *(Our baptisms may appear quite commonplace, but they have the power to change our lives.)*

The rejected and lonely woman was transformed and became a faithful follower filled with joy. *(Just imagine what God can do with all the problems in our lives!)*

She did not tell the townspeople that she had all the answers or knew the "right" truth. She invited them to come and see. *(Sometimes our greatest witness is evident in our manner of actions and not in our words.)*

The disciples returned from town with the food. No one followed. The disciples attended to their own needs and neglected to invite the townspeople to "come and see." Jesus declined the disciples' food. The Samaritan woman proved to be a better evangelist than his own disciples. We should never take our own relationships with God for granted. It is important to share the good news with others.

We never discover this woman's name, yet we know more about her than half of the "regular" disciples. Because of her, we do know that Jesus has the power to transform lives. As the baptized people of God, we become part of the living water that refreshes the world. This water washes away barriers and unifies God's people.

Reflection Questions

1. This hymn is composer Sir Henry Baker's dying confession of faith. What words comprise our confessions of faith? Do our lives proclaim this message?

The King of love my Shepherd is, Whose goodness faileth never,
  I nothing lack if I am His, And He is mine forever.
Where streams of living water flow. My ransomed soul He leadeth,
  And where the verdant pastures grow, With food celestial feedeth.
Perverse and foolish oft I strayed, But yet in love He sought me,
  And on His shoulder gently laid, And home, rejoicing, brought me.
(1869)

2. Jesus approached the Samaritan woman who had been rejected by others. Who can we reach in Christ's name?

3. We must each be intentional about our discipleship. This women actively sought answers from Jesus. She had a deep desire to learn. How do you continue to grow in the faith?

24

Thomas

Read: John 20:19-29

Background

On Easter Sunday Jesus appeared to the disciples and proclaimed the good news of the Resurrection. The disciple Thomas was not there. He had to wait a full week before he was able to see Christ for himself. Historically, Thomas has been held up to significant criticism. He's been called a "doubting Thomas," a term applied to anyone who is skeptical or untrusting.

The twenty-first of December is the historical festival of St. Thomas. It's the day of the winter solstice, the year's longest night and shortest day. Thomas is remembered this day because he was the last of the apostles to be convinced of Jesus' resurrection and thereby had the longest night of unbelief and doubt.

Over the years people have associated Thomas with those who were incomplete, needed help, were last, or were all alone. In Germany, the *Domesel* or *Thomasfaulpelz* ("the lazy bone" or "donkey of St. Thomas Day") were names given to the last person to get out of bed or for the last student to appear in class on December 21.

In historic England, the festival of St. Thomas was a day of charity; the poor went a "Thomasing" or begging. Thomas was the patron saint of those in need. Food was cooked and distributed for the poor. The genteel beggars would give their benefactors a sprig of holly. The following verse was sung:

Christmas is coming; the goose is getting fat,
Please put a penny in the old man's hat.
If you haven't got a penny, half-a-penny will do.
If you haven't got half-a-penny, God bless you!

Thomas is mentioned as a disciple in all four Gospels. He was considered neither the most nor the least important of the twelve disciples. We first hear from Thomas in the eleventh chapter of John's Gospel. Jesus and the disciples have just been told that Lazarus is dead. In order to visit the family, they must first go to Jerusalem. Threats have been made and they know Jerusalem is not safe. Thomas doesn't hesitate and shows courage by saying, "Come along. We might as well die with him" (11:16).

During the preparation for the Last Supper, Thomas asked, "Lord, we do not know where you are going. How can we know the way?" Jesus said, "I am the way, and the truth, and the life. No one comes to the Father except through me. If you know me, you will know my Father also. From now on you do know him and have seen him" (John 14:5-7).

The way that Jesus spoke of is not some geographical location on a map. It is a description of God's revelation in Jesus. To know "the way" is the same as knowing Jesus himself. Thomas' question resulted in an important faith message for us all.

Thomas was absent when the Risen Lord appeared to the other apostles on the first Easter day. He refused to believe that Christ had risen until he saw for himself. When he had seen the Risen Savior he exclaimed, "My Lord and My God!" (John 20:19-29).

Reflections

We all have doubts at times. Doubts raise questions and inspire us to seek answers. The only foolish questions are the ones never asked. To criticize Thomas for having doubts is quite inappropriate. Doubt gives way to faith just as darkness gives way to light. We can, however, criticize Thomas for turning away from the fellowship of believers when he needed them the most. The disciples were afraid and confused. On Good Friday, they lost their Lord and master. On Easter Sunday, the followers of Christ were filled with fear. They gathered together in the same upper room where Jesus had shared the Last Supper. In that special place, the Lord was made known to them again. Christ had risen. Christ had risen indeed. Alleluia!

Thomas was alone in his grief. He missed hearing and seeing the good news. Fellowship is a special gift from God. We come together to share our stories, needs, trials, sorrows, help, and joys. The Risen Lord appeared to a fellowship of believers on Easter morning. Today Christ is made known when we gather as his family and care for each other.

Many early church authors indicate St. Thomas eventually preached in India. Today we celebrate the life of Thomas for the questions he asked and for showing us the importance of fellowship. His story is known throughout the world.

Reflection Questions

1. St. Francis of Assisi (1181-1226) wrote the following prayer. He struggled with doubts during the violent crusades and later found God's peace. What is the importance of faith? Joy? Love? Pardon? Giving? Peace? Eternal Life?

Lord, make me an instrument of your peace.
Where there is hatred, let me sow love. Where there is injury, pardon.
Where there is doubt, faith. Where there is despair, hope.
Where there is darkness, light. Where there is sadness, joy.
Grant that I may not so much seek to be consoled as to console,
To be understood as to understand, to be loved, as to love,
For it's in giving that we receive, and it's in pardoning that we are pardoned,
And it's in dying that we are born to eternal life.

2. Why do some Christians avoid going to church or participating in activities? What are they missing? What can we do to welcome them?

3. The secret of finding meaningful answers is usually asking significant questions. Do you spend sufficient time in search of God's truth? What more can you do?

25

James

Read: Mark 10:35-45

Background

Little is known of James outside of references that include his brother John. James was the elder son of Zebedee who owned a fishing boat on the Sea of Galilee. James and John were called to follow Jesus to "fish" for people to be followers of Jesus. They obeyed.

Peter, James, and John were part of Jesus' inner circle. They were present when:

Jesus raised the daughter of Jairus from the dead (Mark 5; Luke 8).

Jesus was transfigured (Matthew 17; Mark 9; Luke 9).

Jesus went to pray in the Garden of Gethsemane (Matthew 26; Mark 14).

James was part of the group that asked about signs of the end times. Jesus told them:

> As for yourselves, beware; for they will hand you over to councils; and you will be beaten in synagogues; and you will stand before governors and kings because of me, as a testimony to them. And the good news must first be proclaimed to all nations. When they bring you to trial and hand you over, do not worry beforehand about what you are to say; but say whatever is given you at that time, for it is not you who speak, but the Holy Spirit. (Mark 13:8-10)

Jesus certainly didn't pull any punches. He told them the way it was. He warned his closest disciples that ministry was not always easy. This greatest mission in life would require total commitment; there would be no room in heaven for part-time Christians!

James and John one day asked if they could have a special place of honor when Jesus came into his kingdom. The other disciples were angered by this attempt to gain privilege. Jesus responded, "Whoever wishes to become great among you must be your servant, and whoever wishes to be first among you must be slave of all" (Mark 10:43-44).

James' solo moment of mention was in his death. "About that time King Herod laid violent hands upon some who belonged to the church. He had James, the brother of John, killed with the sword." (Acts 12:1-3).

James' early martyrdom signified that he was an important leader in the early church. He paid the ultimate price for his devotion to the Christ. Later, Clement of Alexandria wrote that James repeated Jesus' words on the cross and forgave his accusers.

Reflections

James originally asked for a special place in Jesus' kingdom, and ultimately James was first in Christ's kingdom. He asked for special consideration, and he was the first disciple to lose his life in service for Christ. James was the first to drink his master's cup of sacrifice and to be baptized with his master's baptism of suffering.

James is the only disciple whose death is officially recorded in Scripture. We rely on traditions from the early church for details about the twelve apostles who were all willing to sacrifice their lives for Christ. These traditions suggest the following about the disciples:

Andrew—crucified.

Bartholomew—whipped, beaten, and then crucified.

James, son of Alphaneus—stoned to death.

James, son of Zebedee—beheaded.

Judas (not Iscariot)—stoned to death.

Matthew—speared to death.

Peter—crucified upside down.

Philip—crucified.

Simon—crucified.

Thomas—speared to death.

Matthias (who replaced Judas Iscariot)—stoned to death.

John—poisoned, survived, and later imprisoned.

Tradition indicates John, James' brother, was the only disciple to die a natural death. John was the only disciple who followed Jesus all the way to the cross. John stood at the foot of the cross and heard his master's command, "Behold, your mother," as Jesus committed his mother, Mary, to his care (John 19:26-27).

There is a great paradox in the fact that these same disciples were the ones who were afraid and hid in the upper room early Easter morning. What event in history could have caused these men filled with fear to become bold witnesses with no fear of death? The resurrection transformed them and at Pentecost the Holy Spirit came to empower them.

The Apostle Paul would later write: "For I am convinced that neither death, nor life, nor angels, nor rulers, nor things present, nor things to come, nor powers, nor height, nor depth, nor anything else in all creation, will be able to separate us from the love of God in Christ Jesus our Lord!" (Romans 8:38-39). Paul, too, courageously challenged death for Christ. Encountering the Risen Lord changes lives forever. Thanks be to God!

Reflection Questions

1. Earl Bowman Marlatt experienced loss as a WWI artillery officer. Later, as a Perkins School of Theology professor, he wrote this hymn about James. Can you answer Christ's question?

"Are ye able," said the Master, "To be crucified with Me?"
"Yea," the sturdy dreamers answered, "To the death we follow Thee."
Lord, we are able. Our spirits are Thine.
Remold them, make us, like Thee, divine.
Thy guiding radiance above us shall be
A beacon to God, to love and loyalty. (1926)

2. The word *martyr* translated means "witness." What does it mean to be a witness for Christ today? What hardships are we asked to endure? Are you willing?

3. The Bible compares trials in our lives to a refiner's fire that burns away impurities. How have personal struggles increased your spiritual strength? How would you describe your Christian character?

26

Pontius Pilate

Read: John 18:28-38

Background

Pontius Pilate may be one of the most famous villains in history. Millions of Christians recite the Apostle's Creed professing, "I believe in Jesus Christ, his only Son, our Lord. He was conceived by the power of the Holy Spirit and born of the Virgin Mary. He suffered under Pontius Pilate, was crucified, died, and was buried."

Numerous historic artifacts and writings confirm the role of Pontius Pilate:

Antonio Frova, Italian archaeologist, in 1961 discovered a monument with Pontius Pilate's name inscribed on it at the Mideast city of Caesarea on the Sea.

Cornelius Tacitus (circa AD 55 to 117) was a historian and high-ranking Roman official who served as governor of the Roman provinces in Asia. Tacitus wrote of the execution of Jesus by Pontius Pilate in the reign of Tiberius.

Philo of Alexandria (circa 20 BC to AD 50) was considered the greatest Jewish philosopher of his time. He condemned Pilate for rape, insult, murder, and inhumanity.

The Gospel of John contains the most detailed description of Pilate and his actions. In typical Johannine fashion, the story unfolds in seven scenes. Each scene reveals the character of Pontius Pilate. He had an opportunity to pardon Jesus, knowing him to be guiltless, but he caved in to the demands of the people.

Scene 1: Jesus is brought before Pilate. Charges are made. Pilate tries to pass the buck and tells the religious authorities to "judge him according to your own law." They refuse. They surrender spiritual authority to Rome to punish a man who preached religious freedom.

Scene 2: Pilate asks Jesus, "Are you the King of the Jews?" Jesus answers the question with a question. Pilate's response shows a disdain for those in his charge. Jesus is the good shepherd who cared for all. Pilate doesn't understand benevolent leadership.

Scene 3: Pilate tries to use Barabbas to free Jesus. Pilate avoids making the right decision by hoping the religious leaders will choose the lesser of two evils. Barabbas is described as a "bandit." This is the same word Jesus used to describe those who threaten the good shepherd's sheep (John 10:1-8). The crowd chooses to free the real criminal. Pilate's plan fails.

Scene 4: Jesus is flogged. Pilate hopes the violent punishment will be sufficient. Jesus is mocked and called "King of the Jews." This is an insult against those pushing for his execution. The ploy fails. Jesus must suffer on the cross.

Scene 5: Pilate declares, *"Ecce Homo"* (Here Is the Man!). Pilate judges Jesus. Pilate is guilty of permitting the murder. Pilate demonstrates that he is not a man of courage.

Scene 6: Jesus says those who "handed me over or betrayed me" did the greater sin. Judas betrayed Jesus. The religious leaders handed Jesus over to Pilate who handed him over to the soldiers for crucifixion. They are guilty but Jesus is condemned.

Scene 7: Pilate is reminded that his first priority should be loyalty to the emperor. Pilate states, "Here is your King" and surrenders Jesus. Ironically, Pilate inadvertently put Jesus on the Roman judge's seat (right where he belongs!). Jesus will ultimately preside at the last judgment.

The religious leaders complete the tragedy by declaring that their lives are dedicated to serving the emperor. In that moment they reject God's rule. The drama is complete. An innocent man is condemned to death.

Reflections

Historically some people have blamed all Jewish people for Jesus' death. That is categorically wrong. The Gospel of John makes it very clear that only a handful of powerful religious leaders manipulated the situation. They used Pilate's past indiscretions against him. Pilate showed his cowardice by quickly caving in.

Any religious leader who neglects personal responsibility for private gain goes against the will of God. This offense is not limited to any one religion or denomination. Every organization, including the church, is led by imperfect people. Institutions will never be totally free of corruption because people run them. That is why we all need a savior. We must always fight the temptation to do things our way.

Many religious leaders are very gifted people. The Gospels instruct, "To whom much has been given, much will be required" (Luke 12:48). Jesus was the Good Shepherd. He showed us a model of loving and caring leadership. He fought the good fight.

Pilate tried to avoid personal responsibility. He tried to manipulate the situation and asserted his own blamelessness in the proceeding. He took no responsibility. He was willing to sacrifice an innocent to avoid conflict.

Sometimes we turn away from the truth and avoid doing the right thing because we have misplaced our trust or lost sight of our real purpose—to abide in the love and grace of God.

Reflection Questions

1. Emily Dickinson (1830-1886) sought a reflective life, not a public one (her father was a rich member of Congress). Bible and hymn verses inspired her. Her quest for truth was a life's journey. Consider these verses. What's the only crown we should care about?

One crown that no one seeks. And yet the highest head.
Its isolation coveted. Its stigma deified.
While Pontius Pilate lives. In whatsoever hell.
That coronation pierces him. He recollects it well.

2. Why is it important to take personal responsibility in times of conflict? Consider some examples of those who have. What difference does it make?

3. Martin Luther said, "My temptations have been my masters in divinity." How can we grow in the midst of trials? How does God help us? How can we help one another?

27

The Devil

Read: Luke 4:1-13

Background

He is known as the devil (from the Greek *diabolos* meaning "the slanderer"), Satan ("the adversary"), Beelzebub ("lord of the flies"), Lucifer ("false light"), prince of darkness, accuser, the evil one, deceiver, great dragon, father of lies, god of the world, the tempter, and the ancient serpent.

The Bible reveals that the evil one is the temporary ruler of this world who wages battle against goodness and God. The devil instigates pain and suffering and then encourages us to blame God for the world's imperfections.

The devil used his main methods of temptation in the wilderness story. Since Jesus was alone in his struggle with the tempter, he must have shared these details with his followers to prepare them for their own struggles with Satan.

This "wilderness" probably refers to the vast wasteland desert of Judea that stretched eastward from the highlands around Jerusalem down to the Jordan River and the Dead Sea. The terrain was dry and desolate and dotted with sharp, jagged rocks. The bare limestone and yellow sand glowed with heat like a vast furnace.

While alone in the wilderness, Satan tempted Jesus in the following three ways:

The **first temptation** with the bread required Jesus to perform a selfish miracle. Jesus could have used miracles to bribe others to follow him. He didn't. Jesus only performed miracles for the Glory of God. We should never use our God-given gifts for selfish reasons.

Jesus answered the tempter with the very words that God taught the people of Israel during the Exodus in the desert: "One does not live by bread alone, but by every word that comes from the mouth of the LORD" (Deuteronomy 8:3).

The **second temptation** was to give Jesus all authority over the kingdoms of the earth. This was a hollow offer. Jesus already had God's authority. God empowers those who believe.

This temptation comes at a great price. Jesus need only worship the devil. Jesus quoted Scripture that tells us to worship and serve only God (Deuteronomy 6:13).

The **third temptation** took place on top of the Jerusalem temple. There a priest announced with trumpet the beginning of morning worship daily at dawn. The tempter misquoted Scripture and encouraged Jesus to throw himself off that temple. That would force God's angels to protect him. Jesus would have been an overnight sensation. Such an act would attract attention but would not glorify God's kingdom. God wants us to take risks for the sake of the kingdom and not for our own sake.

Jesus quoted "the Shema" which was Israel's confession of faith: "The LORD is our God, the LORD alone. You shall love the LORD your God with all your heart, and with all your soul, and with all your might" (Deuteronomy 6:4-9).

Many faithful Jews, at the beginning and end of each day, recited these words. Jesus ended the temptations by showing Scripture can be our comfort during spiritual struggles.

Reflections

The temptations reaffirm that Jesus was fully divine and fully human. Jesus struggled just as we do. He was tempted in every way that we are, so he understands our struggles. Jesus showed how we can resist Satan by focusing our attention on God's Word.

Auguste Rodin is famous for his public sculptures, including "The Thinker." He made two companion pieces called "The Hands of God" and "The Hands of the Devil." The first portrays two strong hands forming a spirited man and woman from a lifeless lump of clay. The second looks like the same hands but they are purposely intent on destroying any shape or meaning.

The devil shows a willingness to adapt, improvise, and to overcome. The devil looks for subtle ways to tempt, deceive, and destroy us each and every day. We find comfort and direction in worship and God's Holy Word.

Temptation is not a punishment for being human. It should be a force that drives us into God's loving arms. Giving in to temptation furthers human glory. Defeating temptation advances God's glory.

The tempter visited Jesus at Caesarea Philippi when Peter tried to convince Jesus not to follow the way of the cross. Jesus said to Simon Peter the same words he said to the tempter in the wilderness, "Get behind me, Satan" (Matthew 16:23). Jesus eventually rejected the tempter for all time in the Garden of Gethsemane.

C. S. Lewis' book *The Screwtape Letters* mockingly portrays the devil as spending his time convincing us he doesn't exist so that he can get away with more havoc. The devil encourages us to do too little or too much on our own. We ignore "God's way" and want to do things "our way." The devil's hymn of praise could be "I did it my way."

Reflection Questions

1. Gregory the Great (AD 540-604) was the first monk ever to become pope. He initiated worship renewal based on Scripture. What makes the forty days of Jesus' temptation glorious? How can wilderness experiences be positive times of growth?

The glory of these forty days, we celebrate with songs of praise;
For Christ, by Whom all things were made, himself has fasted and has prayed.
Alone and fasting Moses saw, the loving God Who gave the law;
And to Elijah, fasting, came the steeds and chariots of flame.
Then grant us, Lord, like them to be, full oft in fast and prayer with Thee;
Our spirits strengthen with Thy grace, and give us joy to see Thy face.

2. During the Lord's Prayer we say "Lead us not into temptation." This has also been translated as "Save us from the time of trial." What does this mean?

3. How does Satan misuse Scripture today? How can we fight back?

28

Luke

Read: Luke 1:1–4

Background

The symbol for Luke the Evangelist is an ox (see above). The author of Luke's Gospel is now widely thought to be the author of the book of Acts as well. Both books are addressed to "Theophilus" (which means "lover of God") who may have been a Roman nobleman. Together these two books (there are twenty-seven books in the New Testament) make up more than 27 percent of the entire New Testament text. Luke is the longest Gospel, and Acts provides a comprehensive history of the early Christian church.

It is ironic that the book of Acts contains significant historical information, but we are uncertain about many details regarding Luke the person.

Some early writings state that Luke was born a slave in Antioch, Syria. Wealthy families commonly sent favored slaves to medical school for training. Occasionally these slaves were rewarded freedom for outstanding service. We know Luke was a gifted person. Paul refers to Luke as "the beloved physician" (Colossians 4:14).

We're not certain how Luke and Paul met and became partners in ministry. There was a large university with a medical school in Tarsus. It was considered one of the best in the world. Some suggest Luke met Paul in Tarsus. Later, Paul sought out this old friend and shared the good news.

Luke is mentioned in three other books (Colossians 4:14; 2 Timothy 4:11; Philemon 1:24). Most scholars include him in the famous "we" sections (Acts 16:10-17; Acts 20:5-15; Acts 27:1-37; Acts 28:1-14) that describe adventures with Paul on the second and third missionary journeys. These could have been from Luke's very own spiritual journal.

Other accounts state that Luke was a disciple of the apostles, followed Paul until his death, was single, and died at the age of eighty-four filled with the Holy Spirit.

The Gospel of Luke and the book of Acts do provide us with several clues about Luke. He was:

Multicultural. Church tradition indicates Luke was a Gentile. Paul supports this by grouping Luke's name with other known Gentiles (Colossians 4). Luke had a special heart for accepting people from other cultures. Luke's message of Christ was meant for all people of all races and nations.

Compassionate. Luke stressed that Jesus cared for the oppressed. Jesus showed concern for children who were rejected or neglected. Women were treated with kindness and great respect. The women were treated like disciples and principal supporters of Jesus and his followers. For Luke, poverty was a virtue: "Blessed are the poor" and "blessed are you who hunger now."

Talented. The Gospel of Luke and the book of Acts are considered among the best-written books of the Bible. The use of language is outstanding, the historical references invaluable. Luke was a master storyteller and historian (by the standards of his day). His parables and stories are filled with meaningful details.

Spiritual. Only his Gospel contains details like the prodigal son, the good Samaritan, the penitent thief on the cross, Dives and Lazarus, and Zacchaeus. These are all stories of God's amazing grace. There is a special emphasis on prayer: Jesus prayed at his baptism, at the transfiguration, and at the calling of the disciples.

Artistic. He quoted divine poetry in his historical hymns of Zechariah ("Blessed be the Lord God of Israel"), Mary ("My soul magnifies the Lord"), and Simeon ("Lord, now let your servant depart in peace.")

Reflections

The name *Luke* means "bringer of light." His ministry and writings continue to bring light to our world. He lived out the words of Jesus, "To whom much is given, of him much is expected" (Luke

12:48). Luke was a talented servant of God whose work continues to transform people's lives today.

A survey of the key themes in Luke's Gospel provide us with a guide for Christian living. In Luke, there is a clear concern for the poor, starting with the words of Mary's song in Luke 1 ("he has filled the hungry with good things," verse 53) and announced in Jesus' first public sermon in Luke 4 ("The Spirit of the Lord . . . has anointed me to bring good news to the poor," verse 18). Also, the message of the good news of Jesus is understood to be meant for all people. His emphasis on prayer and on the guidance of the Holy Spirit are also evident in both Luke and Acts.

Though we know little about him as a person, his words provide a powerful message. His remarkable two-volume gift to the church has brought the gospel story to millions of people. How do our lives and words bring light to the gospel for others?

Reflection Questions

1. Adelaide Pollard wanted to be a missionary but could not raise the funds on her own. She wrote this hymn as a fervent prayer. God's will was done. She raised the funds needed. What is God's way? How does God touch us? Heal us? Mold us?

> Have Thine own way, Lord! Have Thine own way! Thou art the Potter, I am the clay.
>
> Mold me and make me after Thy will, while I am waiting, yielded and still.
>
> Have Thine own way, Lord! Have Thine own way! Wounded and weary, help me, I pray!
>
> Power, all power, surely is Thine! Touch me and heal me, Savior divine. (1907)

2. It is important to keep a journal of your faith journey. How have Luke's writings benefited us? How can we benefit others? Write on!

3. PBPGINFWMY stands for "Please Be Patient; God Is Not Finished With Me Yet." Consider the highs and lows of your spiritual journey. Share them with others. Why is patience so important?

29
Mary Magdalene

Read: Matthew 28:1-10

Background

Mary Magdalene, a woman healed by Jesus, went on to play an important role as a follower of Christ. Mary is mentioned fourteen times in Scripture and referred to in all four Gospels. She also became an easy target for poets, priests, painters, and performing artists. For fourteen-hundred years, Mary Magdalene has been portrayed as the prostitute who was transformed by Jesus. She's called the patron saint of fallen women.

Mary was from the seaside town of Magdala (which means "tower") located on the coast of Galilee. We don't know much about Magdala because it was completely destroyed by the Romans before the Gospels were written. Luke introduces her this way: "The twelve were with him, as well as some women who had been cured of evil spirits and infirmities: **Mary, called Magdalene, from whom seven demons had gone out,** and Joanna, the wife of Herod's steward Chuza, and Susanna, and many others, who provided for them out of their resources" (Luke 8:2-3).

We simply do not know the nature of the seven demons that Jesus cast out of Mary Magdala. There are references to Jesus healing people with demons, who had epileptic seizures (Matthew 17:15-19), were mute (Matthew 9:32-33), were blind (Matthew 12:22), hurt themselves (Mark 5:5), attacked others (Matthew 8:28), or spoke nonsense (John 8:49-53). These so-called demons could have simply been any combination of mental or physical afflictions.

We do know Jesus healed Mary Magdalene. Over the years, many have seen her as an easy target for unsubstantiated allegations. For example, Pope Gregory the Great preached an Easter sermon (AD 591) in which he proclaimed, "She whom Luke calls the sinful woman, whom John calls Mary, we believe to be Mary from whom seven devils were ejected, according to Mark. And what did these seven devils signify, if not all the vices? . . . It is clear that the woman previously used the same ointment to perfume her flesh in forbidden acts."

Gregory identified Mary's seven demons as the seven universal "human vices." He grouped them together and called them the seven cardinal sins (lust, greed, envy, gluttony, anger, laziness, pride). Gregory was mistaken. There is nothing in Scripture that connects Mary of Magdalene with the other women cited. In 1969, the Second Vatican Council apologized and declared her a saint. She is "the one to whom Christ appeared after the Resurrection." Recent scholarship has helped restore Mary Magdalene's name and reputation, but old habits die hard.

To set the record straight, Mary Magdalene made many significant contributions:

Her name is often listed first among the women who followed Jesus. Her name carries the same respect afforded Peter whose name was always first among disciples.

She was a woman of wealth. She helped support Jesus and his disciples, a common practice. Mary's support enabled Jesus to travel and teach.

While most disciples abandoned Jesus, Mary Magdalene had the courage to follow him all the way to Calvary. She stood beside his mother, Mary, the entire time.

She cared for Jesus after his death. She helped at his burial.

She was the first to see the resurrected savior on Easter morning. She ran to tell the disciples the "good news."

Saint Augustine called Mary Magdalene "the apostle to the Apostles." Jesus commissioned Mary to tell the disciples where he was going. The disciples did not listen and rejected her message. They should have paid attention. She knew the world's greatest news ever!

Reflections

Contemporary fiction has complicated Mary's image by asserting she was married to Jesus. This is sensationalism and absolute nonsense. Any serious student of the Bible or Christian history can quickly discount these fabrications.

We should all learn from Gregory's mistake. We should ignore the petty lies and pay attention to the truth Mary proclaimed on Easter morning. Mary was truly the first apostle. Jesus sent her to announce the resurrection.

Jesus gave Mary a very special task in the kingdom. When we dismiss Mary (or make false allegations) we ignore Christ's transforming power. Jesus heals us and sends us out to share the good news. Rich or poor, male or female, sick or healthy, Jesus values us all.

Reflection Questions

1. Franciscan Friar Jean Tisserand was known for his caring ministry to troubled men and women of the street. He shared Easter joy with this hymn. How has the grave lost its sting? Why were the women faithful? Was Mary a child of the king? Are you?

Sons and daughters of the King, Whom heavenly hosts in glory sing,
Today the grave has lost its sting! Alleluia! Alleluia, alleluia,
  alleluia!
That Easter morn, at break of day, The faithful women went their
  way
To seek the tomb where Jesus lay. Alleluia! Alleluia, alleluia, alleluia!
An angel clad in white they see, Who sits and speaks unto the three,
"Your Lord will go to Galilee." Alleluia! Alleluia, alleluia, alleluia!
(1494)

2. God creates, saves, calls, and commands us to serve God. How did Mary fulfill her assignment? How do you fulfill yours?

3. It was a common practice in Jesus' day for a woman or man of means to support religious leaders. How do we support Jesus' work today? Why do our donations make such a big difference for the work of the kingdom?

30

The Good Samaritan

Read: Luke 10:25-37

Background

One day a religious lawyer came to test Jesus. He asked the master, "What must I do to obtain eternal life?" Jesus answered with another question. He asked, "What do the Scriptures instruct you to do?" Jesus challenged "the expert" to provide an answer.

The man responded, "You shall love the Lord your God with all your heart, and with all your soul, and with all your strength, and with all your mind; and your neighbor as yourself." This was a quote from the *Shema* (Deuteronomy 6).

The legal expert asked Jesus, "Who is my neighbor?" The word *neighbor* means "one who is near." He was asking Jesus "who is close enough to me that I must respond in love?" Jesus answered with a parable, a story that reveals a clear truth.

One day a man was traveling from Jerusalem to Jericho. His race, religion, or nationality is never mentioned. The seventeen-mile journey was a difficult one. The narrow road was steep, rugged, and rocky. Bandits attacked and robbed the man and left him for dead.

A priest who presided over the sacrifices at the Temple that atoned for people's sins just passed by. A Levite who served in God's temple also passed by. It is possible both men avoided the victim because they were concerned about ritual purity. This argument is weakened because the next traveler saw that the victim was still breathing. Jewish law taught "saving a life" overruled any other regulation (Babylonian Talmud, Yoma 82a).

Jesus surprised his audience by revealing it was a Samaritan who helped the man. In Jesus' day the Jews and Samaritans mistrusted each other. The Samaritans had their own temple and their own priests. Many Jewish people considered Samaritans to be spiritual enemies. So it was likely shocking when Jesus described the Samaritan as the one who saw the man and was filled with compassion.

The Samaritan acted out of love and compassion: "He **went** to him and **bandaged** his wounds, and **poured** oil and wine on them. Then he **put** him on his own animal, **brought** him to an inn, and **took care** of him." The next day he followed with further action by **giving** the landlord two silver coins (enough for a week's lodging) and **guaranteed** payment of further expenses.

The Samaritan had exceeded all required duty. There was an extravagance about his love of neighbor. He gave freely of his possessions, medicines, transportation, and compassion. He loved his neighbor as he loved himself.

Jesus then asked the legal expert, "Which of these three, do you think, was a neighbor to the man who fell into the hands of the robbers?" The man who sought to trap Jesus found himself ensnared. He could not bring himself to say "the Samaritan" so he responded, "The one who showed him mercy." Jesus concluded, "Go and do likewise!"

Reflections

Jesus exceeded expectations in this story by breaking down all boundaries of race, religion, and nationality. Jesus demonstrated that being legally righteous is not the same as loving one's neighbor. The parable shows us that we are no longer slaves because we have found perfect freedom in Christ.

Dr. Martin Luther King Jr.'s final sermon, delivered the night before he was assassinated, was based on this story. In his famous "I've Been to the Mountaintop" sermon, Dr. King encouraged his audience to overcome fear and develop "a kind of dangerous unselfishness."

Dr. King considered the two men who saw the wounded man. They thought it was too dangerous to stop and help. Possibly they thought the bandits were still nearby. Possibly they thought, "If I stop to help this man, what will happen to me?"

The Samaritan reversed the question. He exhibited a dangerous kind of unselfishness. He asked himself the question, "If I do not stop to help this man, what will happen to him?" That's the right question. It's not about me! That's love of neighbor. Jesus tells us to "Go and do likewise!"

Martin Luther King Jr. had the courage needed to help those in need, and he gave his life helping others. Jesus said, "No greater love has a man than to lay down his life for another" (John 15:13). Jesus led by example. Dr. King followed. How might we do the same?

Reflection Questions

1. Rev. Frank Mason North ministered to the urban poor during tough economic times. These words capture needs that still exist today. Who is our neighbor? What can we do? Why?

> Where cross the crowded ways of life, where sound the cries of race
>   and clan,
> above the noise of selfish strife, we hear thy voice, O Son of Man.
> In haunts of wretchedness and need, on shadowed thresholds dark
>   with fears,
> from paths where hide the lures of greed, we catch the vision of thy
>   tears.
> Till all the world shall learn thy love, and follow where thy feet
>   have trod;
> till glorious from thy heaven above, shall come the city of our God.
> (1903)

2. What kinds of hopes, interests, ambitions, dreams, and affections do you have for the work of the gospel? What are you doing about it?

3. What kind of life is even better than the "good life"? Or framed another way: What makes life truly good?

31

The Rich Young Ruler

Read: Mark 10:17-26

Background

Understanding this story is like fitting together pieces of a puzzle. Matthew, Mark, and Luke all tell the same story, yet each writer presents different viewpoints about the main character. Mark mentions he is rich. Matthew states he is young. Luke adds he is a ruler. Together they tell the whole story.

One day this rich young ruler runs up to Jesus asking, "What must I do to have **eternal life**?" He rushed to ask the question but was slow to accept Jesus' answer.

It's important to understand the term *eternal life* is not limited to the hereafter with God. Eternal life also refers to an immediate fullness of life with God. The term incorporates the future and present simultaneously. This young man may have had an eye toward the future but he wanted a purpose-filled life, now! He even went beyond the letter of the law and loved both God and neighbor. Yet, he was anxious. Something was missing. He begged Jesus for an answer. He was asking "What more can I do?"

He may have anticipated that Jesus would give him just one more commandment. Carry out just one more accomplishment and his life would be complete. But Jesus' answer was more than he expected. Jesus instructed him to do three things:

sell everything you have;

give everything away to the poor (you will have treasure in heaven); and

come (follow me).

Jesus invited him to leave everything behind and become a disciple. He'd obtain the world's greatest treasure when he gave up the world's riches. Jesus' response reflected the values of God's kingdom. The rich young ruler could help those in need. Disciples were called to help widows, orphans, children, the hungry, the naked, and the imprisoned.

The rich young ruler just couldn't do it. He could not accept Jesus' invitation to be a generous disciple. He was filled with sadness and left. Jesus was filled with sadness too. Here was a man who could have been a great leader in the Christian church. He could have written another gospel. He could have shared in the glory of Christ's kingdom.

Jesus concluded that it was easier for a camel to pass through the eye of the needle than for a rich man to get into heaven. This is confusing imagery. There are a number of possible interpretations:

The original word for "camel" is just one vowel away from the word for "rope." Did someone misspell the word? Mark's grammar was not always the best.

Others maintain there was a low gate in Jerusalem called "the eye of the needle." Entry through this gate required camels to get down on their knees. Could this mean that rich people need to be humbled in order to gain entry into God's kingdom?

Or perhaps Jesus was simply saying: Those who trust in riches cannot trust in God. No one can serve two masters.

Reflections

The twelve disciples followed when Jesus called them. The rich young ruler could not. Initially, he was so eager to find his purpose in life. He came, he saw, and money conquered him. He left dragging his feet because he could not accept Christ's answer.

The rich young ruler thought he had it all. The poor are considered great in God's kingdom. God did not create the world with poverty in mind. God wants us to share with those in need. When we acknowledge that God is our creator, we accept that all people are children of God. We are called to care for our brothers and sisters.

The paradox of the kingdom is that by surrendering our way of life, we can find the true way. Jesus reminds us that he is "the way, the truth, and the life." What are your riches? Possessions? Talents? Abilities? Experience? Faith?

Johann Sebastian Bach is considered to be one of the greatest musicians in history. He was a gifted genius. He was rich in talent. He was also a humble servant of the Lord. He dedicated his life to working for the church. At the top of every composition, he wrote "To the Glory of God." What kind of music are you making with your life? Is God glorified?

Reflection Questions

1. Anglican author Bishop William How served in London's poorest section. He wrote this hymn to be sung while offerings were presented during worship. Who really owns our possessions?

We give Thee but Thine own, whate'er the gift may be;
All that we have is Thine alone, a trust, O Lord, from Thee.
May we Thy bounties thus, as stewards true receive,
And gladly, as Thou blessest us, to Thee our first fruits give. (1864)

2. How can we be a "kingdom builder"? How is kingdom building related to "wealth building"? Why should we care?

3. How might you respond to the challenge Jesus set before the rich young ruler?

32

Lazarus and the Rich Man

Read: Luke 16:19-31

Background

The story of a poor man named Lazarus and a rich man reads like a drama with strong character profiles.

In **Act One,** not a word is spoken but the scene is set and characters identified:

There once was a rich man . . .

The parable never really tells us his name. Tradition indicates his name was "Dives," but that's just the Latin word for "rich," "opulent," or "wealthy."

The man's wealth was great. His purple clothes indicated he was rich or royalty. The cost of just one robe exceeded the average man's annual wage.

He feasted in luxury all day, every day. He enjoyed expensive exotic dishes. In doing so he broke the commandment to work six days and rest on the Sabbath.

He had a gate (for privacy or security) that separated him from everyone else, particularly the needy of the city.

He's not described as evil. He simply never noticed anyone with needs at his doorstep. This rich man is described as "an abomination in the sight of God" (Luke 16:15).

The rich man could have saved Lazarus. He did nothing.

There was a poor man named Lazarus . . .

He was a crippled beggar lying in the street at the gate of the rich man.

His body was covered with open sores. He was so weak that dogs tormented him by licking his wounds (the same dogs that abundantly fed at the master's table).

He was starving. Jesus said, "When you give a feast, do not invite your friends and rich neighbors. Instead, invite the poor, the crippled, the lame, and the blind" (Luke 14:13-23).

This is the only time a person is given a name in any of Jesus' parables.

The name *Lazarus* means, "God is my help."

In **Act Two,** Lazarus dies of starvation. The rich man unexpectedly dies. The two men never spoke in life and lived separated by a table and a gate. The separation is even greater in death.

Act Three provides the parable's focal point.

In this scene the poor are rich and the rich are poor. Lazarus finds himself at the honored side of Father Abraham. The rich man finds himself in a place of torment.

There are **three** complete exchanges between the rich man and father Abraham; Lazarus never says a word.

The rich man begs for a drop of water. Abraham responds that the roles on earth are now reversed and that it's too late to cross the heavenly divide. There's no indication that the rich man has had a change of heart.

The rich man accepts his fate and begs to warn his five brothers. Abraham refuses and states they can always learn the same lesson from Moses and the prophets.

The rich man argues his brothers will only pay attention to the miracle of someone returning from the dead. Abraham disagrees and declares that anyone who ignores Moses and the prophets will not listen to "someone who rises from the dead" (a hidden reference to Jesus). The story ends (or does it?).

Reflections

We are initially inclined to identify with Lazarus (or the rich man). This parable is much more subtle. In the end, many of us identify with the five remaining brothers. Will we listen to the message of Moses and the prophets that was fulfilled by Jesus Christ?

Dr. Albert Schweitzer's life was changed by this story. He concluded that the poor of Africa were people lying in need at Europe's doorstep. He dedicated his life to service and founded the Lambaréné Hospital. This brought health and salvation to tens of thousands.

Jesus spoke five times more about money, stewardship, and property than about prayer. We cannot serve two masters. We serve God or mammon (possessions), not both.

Before the birth of Jesus, Mary praised God by proclaiming "He has brought down the powerful from their thrones, and lifted up the lowly; he has filled the hungry with good things, and sent the rich away empty. He has helped his servant Israel, in remembrance of his mercy, according to the promise he made to our ancestors, to Abraham and to his descendants forever" (Luke 1:52-55).

The world cries out for those who have been blessed with much to find ways to share their wealth with those who have little. We are all called to look beyond our gates.

Reflection Questions

1. Author Frances Havergal was known for her acts of charity. She practiced what she sang. What do we encourage God to "take" from us? What is your real treasure?

Take my life, and let it be consecrated, Lord, to Thee.
Take my moments and my days; let them flow in ceaseless praise.
Take my silver and my gold; not a mite would I withhold.
Take my intellect, and use every power as Thou shalt choose.
Take my love, my Lord, I pour at Thy feet its treasure store.
Take myself, and I will be ever, only, all for Thee. (1874)

2. Is there someone in need near your home? Around the world? What can you do now?

3. Why do some people spend more time talking about ministry than actually doing it? How and when and where is Jesus calling us into action?

33

Martha and Mary

Read: Luke 10:38-42

Background

It has been said that there are two types of people in the world—those who like to divide the world into two types of people, and those who don't.

Luke's Gospel is filled with pairings that compare and contrast. The tenth chapter has two stories juxtaposed. First is the parable of the Good Samaritan who unexpectedly cares for his neighbor. The second story of Mary and Martha examines traditional forms of service and redefines discipleship.

Martha is described as the formal head of the household. Martha welcomes Jesus and his followers into her home. She busies herself with the responsibility of tending to the guests' needs. Martha simply wants to be a good hostess, but she fails to realize that the disciples are not the only ones whom Jesus will be teaching in her home.

By contrast, **Mary** chooses not help her sister. She sits at the master's feet and listens. Mary assumes an equal role with the other disciples. Mary takes advantage of the opportunity to learn from Jesus. She must learn before she can serve.

Martha becomes quite frustrated. Martha's preoccupations with the tasks at hand blind her to what is really important. Martha interrupts the master's teachings:

She resorts to self-pity.
She becomes angry with others.
She finds fault with others.
She questions God's care.

Martha asks Jesus to send Mary back to the kitchen. Jesus declines Martha's request and gently reprimands her. Jesus welcomes Mary and says she has "chosen the better part." Meals come and go but Mary has chosen the one thing that can never be "taken away from her." Mary opts for the "Chosen One" (Luke 9:35).

Later, when Jesus came to the home of Martha and Mary because of the death of their brother Lazarus, Martha demonstrated a significant change. The sisters were filled with sorrow, but Martha expressed her faith in Jesus, saying, "I believe that you are the Messiah, the Son of God, the one coming into the world" (John 11:27). Martha and Mary followed the Lord together. Jesus raised Lazarus and brought new life to the whole family.

Reflections

Dietrich Bonhoeffer was a courageous champion of the faith. This Lutheran pastor and seminary teacher opposed Hitler and the Nazi movement. The word *martyr* is used to describe someone who is willing to sacrifice his or her life for the sake of the Gospel. Bonhoeffer did just that. His book, *The Cost of Discipleship*, describes the importance of listening. He states that the first service we owe to others in fellowship is to listen to each other. Love of God starts when we listen to God's Word. Our love for each other grows when we listen to each other. We are doing God's work when we listen to God and each other.

Mary listened. When we open ourselves to listening to Jesus we open ourselves to understanding more about him and his role in our lives. Along with Martha we listen for what Jesus has to say about himself:

I am the bread of life (John 6:25).

I am the light of the world (John 9:5).

I am the gate for the sheep (John 10:7).

I am the good shepherd (John 10:11).

I am the resurrection and the life (John 11:25).

I am the way, the truth, and the life (John 14:6).

I am the true vine, and my Father is the vine grower (John 15:1).

By listening to Jesus, Martha was transformed. She no longer majored in the minor details. Jesus shares the foretaste of the feast to come. He is the bread of life (John 6). When we focus on insignificant problems, we come away empty.

Mary had it right from the very beginning. She's mentioned three times in the Gospels and each time she is sitting at the foot of her master. In this story she sat at his feet learning (Luke 10). She fell at the feet of Jesus when he came to help her brother Lazarus (John 11). Mary thanked Jesus by anointing his feet with fragrant oil and cleansing them with her hair (John 12). Mary does not say much, but her actions communicate complete devotion to Christ.

In the end Jesus taught Martha the proper way to welcome a guest. Father Henri Nouwen (religious professor at Notre Dame, Yale, and Harvard) taught that the true meaning of Christian hospitality is creating a space where a visitor can enter in and become a friend. Hospitality means giving the guest an opportunity to give us something in return. Mary and Martha were strengthened by Jesus' visit. So are we.

Reflection Questions

1. Rector John Ernest Bode wrote these words for his own children's confirmation. He spoke to their needs. How can Jesus make us listen? What is the connection between service and listening?

Jesus, I have promised to serve Thee to the end;
Be Thou forever near me, my Master and my Friend;
I shall not fear the battle if Thou art by my side,
Nor wander from the pathway if Thou wilt be my Guide.
O let me hear Thee speaking in accents clear and still,
Above the storms of passion, the murmurs of self-will.
O speak to reassure me, to hasten or control;
O speak, and make me listen, Thou Guardian of my soul. (1868)

2. Being a servant means allowing God to interrupt our schedules at any time. How can we make room for God at all times? What difference does it make?

3. Real servants keep a low profile. What did Martha need to learn from Mary?

34

Zacchaeus

Read: Luke 19:1-10

Background

Jericho was a major metropolitan area known for its fine buildings, wide streets, public squares, and beautiful homes. It was a popular vacation spot because the wintertime was fabulously warm. It was located on major trade routes. Business was very good.

As Jesus entered the city of Jericho, the crowds were great. Many wanted to see this new teacher. Zacchaeus was a very wealthy man because he was the chief tax collector. He was also small in stature and could not see over the crowds.

That day Zacchaeus did two things that influential people never did. He ran ahead (scandalous!) and then climbed up a sycamore tree to see Jesus. The crowd was shocked! Only poor people climbed sycamore trees to get its lowly figs. Zacchaeus had abandoned all pride and stepped out on a limb.

Then there's a twist in the story. While Zacchaeus was trying to see Jesus, Jesus was really seeking Zacchaeus. Jesus invited himself into Zacchaeus' home. Jesus greatly honored Zacchaeus by making this request. This simple act elevated Zacchaeus' community status higher than any climbing could ever accomplish.

Witnessing involves keeping an eye out for those who are looking for a change. Zacchaeus' behavior indicated he was ready for something new. Jesus planned to pass straight through the town of Jericho, but when Jesus saw Zacchaeus' readiness he adjusted his plans. Evangelists need to alter plans at a moment's notice to help when someone is searching.

When Jesus announced he would join Zacchaeus "today," there was immediacy in his statement, and it prompted an immediate response from Zacchaeus. He announced he'd give half his income to the poor and would make amends if he'd ever cheated anyone. The exact translation is confusing. Either Zacchaeus was asking for forgiveness or he was proclaiming his innocence. Either way, Jesus accepted his offer and proclaimed his reputation restored as a true son of Abraham.

Zacchaeus' joy stands in contrast to the crowd's grumbling. Jesus' request was greeted with "murmurs" from the crowd. These were the same type of "murmurs" that occurred in Luke 5:30 and Luke 15:2 when Jesus dined with other tax collectors.

Reflections

Jesus reached out to claim this lost member of God's family. He was willing to show God's outrageous grace and forgiveness. Jesus reminds us that those who think they are perfect have no need of a savior. Zacchaeus humbled himself. He knew he needed help. Salvation found him. The name *Zacchaeus* means "pure." At the end of the day, Jesus Christ cleansed him.

There is an ancient legend that Zacchaeus remained a faithful follower of Jesus. He continued to care for the poor and was honest in his work. He also cared for that special sycamore tree. He watered it daily as a reminder of the day that Jesus recognized and forgave him.

Do you have a sycamore tree in your life? A place where you felt the power of God's love? Maybe it was a special church, a certain program, a church camp, a retreat, or a conference that changed your life. Remember to celebrate and care for your sycamore tree. With your help, that tree can continue to make a difference in someone else's life.

Reflection Questions

1. Consider this selection from Psalm 139. How does God search for us? How does God lead us in the way everlasting?

O LORD, you have searched me and known me.
You know when I sit down and when I rise up; you discern my
*   thoughts from far away.*

You search out my path and my lying down, and are acquainted
  with all my ways.
Even before a word is on my tongue, O LORD, you know it
  completely.
You hem me in, behind and before, and lay your hand upon me.
Such knowledge is too wonderful for me; it is so high that I cannot
  attain it.
Where can I go from your spirit? Or where can I flee from your presence?
If I ascend to heaven, you are there; if I make my bed in Sheol, you
  are there.
Search me, O God, and know my heart; test me and know my thoughts.
See if there is any wicked way in me, and lead me in the way
  everlasting.

2. What has been a "sycamore tree" in your life? Do you still care for it?

3. We all need to find our true identity in Christ. In what ways can we listen to Jesus' message for us? Where do we hear that message?

35
Mark

Read: Acts 15:36-41

Background

The symbol of Mark the Evangelist is the lion of courage (see above). Just who was the writer of Mark's Gospel? Some have identified him as John Mark, the son of the woman named Mary who made her home available to Jesus and his followers (Acts 12:12). Church tradition indicates that Mark served with Peter in Rome when the persecutions of the Christians began. He left Rome after the martyrdoms of Peter and Paul. John Mark went to Alexandria (Egypt) and became its first bishop. He is an honored saint in the Egyptian (Coptic) Church. In AD 832, his bones were taken to Venice (Italy) as a war prize. Today that city honors Mark with a great cathedral and statues of winged lions (his evangelical symbol).

Others have connected the Gospel writer to the Mark mentioned in 1 Peter 5:13, since Peter is mentioned so prominently in the Gospel. For example, early church leader Irenaeus said Mark's Gospel was based on the reminiscences of Peter. He said Peter was the "mind behind" this Gospel. Luke tells us that Peter was an uneducated person. "They saw the boldness of Peter and John and realized that they were uneducated and ordinary men" (Acts 4:13). Peter's story became the Gospel of Mark. Most modern scholars, however, say that it is virtually impossible to identify who "Mark" is.

It has been suggested that Mark's Gospel was written in the decade of AD 65 to 75, during a time when the Christians were suffering persecution at the hands of the Roman emperor Nero. Jesus' warning that the temple in Jerusalem would be destroyed seems to be a reference to the destruction of the Temple by the Romans in AD 70.

Mark wrote in a very simple Greek style, which would have made his Gospel accessible to many readers. He used repetition and other devices to help the hearers recall the message, a message that focused on what Jesus did and who Jesus was. Emphasis is placed on how people identified Jesus. The climax of the Gospel appears to center on the Roman centurion's confession at the foot of the cross: "Truly this man was God's Son!"

Reflections

What must have it been like to be one of the few to write a gospel account of Jesus the Christ? Of all the stories and recollections you would gather in preparing a gospel, which ones do you choose to leave out? How do you organize the material in order to communicate a story that has a great impact on its hearers? What profound purpose one must feel in doing this awesome task!

If you were to put together a simple account of the life of Jesus, what scenes and stories would you include? What is the one single theme you would use to identify Jesus? How would you organize your thoughts? Do you know someone who needs to hear the story? How will you tell it?

The writers of the Gospels are known as evangelists, a term that comes from the Greek word for the gospel (good news). They are tellers of the good news. Each had his own style and approach, but having four different retellings of the story of Jesus is a bonus. We can see Jesus in a four-dimensional way.

When you or others in your church think about sharing the gospel story, think about doing so in a variety of ways. Look for ways to bring depth and dimension to your good news storytelling. You will be enriched, and so will those who come to listen and learn.

Reflection Questions

1. Presbyterian pastor George Duffield courageously dedicated himself to serving struggling congregations. What kind of strength does this hymn convey? What is the source of that power?

Stand up, stand up for Jesus, the trumpet call obey;
Forth to the mighty conflict, in this His glorious day.
Ye that are brave now serve Him against unnumbered foes;
Let courage rise with danger, and strength to strength oppose.
Stand up, stand up for Jesus, stand in His strength alone;
The arm of flesh will fail you, ye dare not trust your own.
Put on the Gospel armor, each piece put on with prayer;
Where duty calls or danger, be never wanting there. (1858)

2. If God only used perfect people, then nothing would ever get done. Have you ever made a mistake in the faith? Did someone help you? Can you help others?

3. Why does it seem to take so much courage to tell others about Jesus? How can you make this a more common part of your life?

36
Paul

Read: Acts 26:12-20

Background

Paul started out in life as "Saul," son of a devout Jew who described himself as "a Hebrew born of Hebrews." He was from Tarsus, one of the largest trade centers on the Mediterranean coast. The influential metropolis was granted special freedoms by Rome. The merchants there were known for quality work and re-investment in community (public works, roads, health, and city beautification). They also sponsored scholars for Tarsus' world-class university.

Paul could have studied philosophy, rhetoric, law, mathematics, astronomy, medicine, geography, botany, athletics, and theater. Roman historian Strabo ranked Tarsus above the prestigious universities of Athens and Alexandria. Athenodorus, Caesar Augustus' teacher, came from Tarsus.

The local mountains were rich in lumber and minerals. Slopes were populated by herds of black goats. Their hair was woven into cloth used in quality cloaks and tents. Travelers across the Mideast used the superior black tents of Tarsus. Rabbinical students often worked skilled jobs to finance their education. Paul was a tentmaker.

Paul went to Jerusalem to study theology under Gamaliel the Elder, a grandson of the renowned Rabbi Hillel. Gamaliel was called "Rabban," which means "our Master" or "Great One." Only seven men in Jewish history ever received this respected title. Paul must have been an exceptional student to study with such a teacher. Gamaliel's nickname was "The Beauty of the Law." He would have taught Paul respect for the law tempered with a concern for the needs of people.

Paul was a well-known defender of Judaism by the age of thirty. He punished Christians (including Stephen) with a passion. Many Christians fled Jerusalem. Paul was empowered to pursue them all the way to Damascus. On one such journey he was blinded by a light from heaven and fell to the ground. He heard Jesus saying, "Saul, Saul, why do you persecute me?"

Paul was transformed. He referred to this call as "a revelation" (Galatians 1:16) and "a new creation" (2 Corinthians 5:17). Paul may have missed seeing Jesus in the flesh, but he witnessed the resurrected Christ on the road to Damascus. Paul's salvation was made possible by the power of God's grace. He called this "justification by faith." His ministry was an ongoing journey in that faith:

• At times Paul did have a short fuse. He sarcastically condemned those who changed Christ's message. He was passionate for the sake of the gospel.

• Paul had a great gift for making friendships. One chapter has a remarkable list of twenty-seven friends and acquaintances (Romans 16).

• Paul knew his own limitations. He referred to the work of Christians as "treasures in earthen vessels" (2 Corinthians 4:7-11). He admitted at times we are like "cracked pots" for the glory of God.

• Paul was willing to take risks. His ministry on Mars Hill (Acts 17) was a creative way to engage people from a different culture and religion.

• Paul celebrated the inner peace and joy of being "in Christ." "I can do all things through him who strengthens me" (Philippians. 4:12-13).

• Church historian Eusebius wrote that Paul was taken to Rome and killed during Nero's persecution in AD 67. Paul had run the good race and Christ was forever the victor.

Reflections

Paul was God's agent of change. The early Christian church had become comfortable in Jerusalem, so growth was slow. Paul helped the church see new possibilities for evangelism. Paul traveled thousands of miles through hostile areas to share the gospel, especially with Gentiles. He was ridiculed, arrested, whipped, beaten, stoned, imprisoned, shipwrecked, and finally martyred. He dedicated his life as a living sacrifice to God's abiding love.

Paul was not perfect, but he is an example of God's power to change. Paul's life purposes were completely reversed. He continued to change throughout his life. He became dedicated to sharing God's message of salvation, forgiveness, grace, righteousness, love, and justification by faith.

His name change to Paul reveals a striking humility. The name *Paul* is Latin for "little," but his impact on the life of the church was, and continues to be, huge. His life-changing encounter with Christ on the Damascus Road led to a change of heart and direction. Sometimes we can get stuck in ruts or get tied up by commitments that do not send us in healthy directions. Sometimes life-changing events break into our lives in a flash, but more often we are aware of the need for change for some time before we seek change.

Discovering our purpose in life has much to do with being open to change and trusting that God will lead, no matter where we are called to go. We can all do big things in our lives to serve the One who calls us to experience life at its fullest. Paul's life and his clear message of gospel truth can inspire and guide us along the way.

Reflection Questions

1. Consider this quote. How does this reflect Paul's life and teachings? Your life?

Who will separate us from the love of Christ? Will hardship, or distress, or persecution, or famine, or nakedness, or peril, or sword? No, in all these things we are more than conquerors through him who loved us. For I am convinced that neither death, nor life, nor angels, nor rulers, nor things present, nor things to come, nor powers, nor height, nor depth, nor anything else in all creation, will be able to separate us from the love of God in Christ Jesus our Lord. (Romans 8:35-39)

2. We are Christ's ambassadors on earth. Paul knew he was a sinner and a saint at the same time. Discuss his shortcomings, his gifts, and his life.

3. Paul was certainly passionate. He sought God's agenda rather than his own. Why has God made every one of us for mission? What can we do about it?

37

Peter

Read: Mark 14:27-31

Background

His name was Simon. He was a fisherman in partnership with Andrew (his brother) and James and John (sons of Zebedee). They fished the northern areas of Lake Galilee. One day Andrew announced he'd found the Messiah and brought Simon to meet Jesus. Jesus called Simon to follow. Later Jesus nicknamed him Cephas (Aramaic for "rock"). This name is also translated as Peter (Latin and Greek for "rock"). Jesus called Peter to be a fisher of men.

Frequently Peter's character resembled shifting sand rather than solid rock. Peter danced a step called the "Simon-bar-Jonah Shuffle." You take one step forward, followed by two steps backward. He would boldly step forward with the right action followed moments later by a retreat.

At Caesarea Philippi, Jesus asked his disciples, "Who do people say that I am?" Peter boldly proclaimed him to be the Christ, the Messiah. Moments later Peter reversed himself by discouraging Jesus from facing the hard times ahead in Jerusalem (Matthew 16:13-20).

The disciples were in a boat in the middle of a storm. Jesus rose above the storm and invited Peter to follow. Peter walked on the water before he lost confidence and sank down (Matthew 14:22-33).

Peter was a bold witness, but at times he talked too much. Peter, James, and John joined Jesus at the Transfiguration. Moses and Elijah joined with Jesus for his final journey to Jerusalem. Peter disrupted the sanctity of the situation by suggesting "booths" to dedicate the sacred space. God's voice declared, "This is my beloved son, listen to him!" Essentially Peter was given a heavenly command to "be quiet" and listen (Luke 9:28-33).

Peter helped John prepare the Last Supper. He refused Jesus' request to wash his feet. Jesus responded, "If I don't wash you, you don't really belong to me." Peter reversed himself and asked Jesus to wash him completely (John 13:1-20).

During the meal Peter pledged his devotion to Jesus. Later, he couldn't stay awake during the prayers in Gethsemane. Jesus later rebuked him (Mark 14:32-42).

Peter followed when Jesus was arrested. He waited in the courtyard outside the high priest's palace. Three times Peter denied knowing Jesus. The rooster crowed and Peter realized he had betrayed his master (Matthew 26:69-75).

When Peter lost sight of Jesus' message, bad things happened. There's a certain contradiction that the name *Simon* means "one who listens." When Peter stepped out of the boat, he was walking on water. He placed his trust in Jesus and rose above the stormy waters of life. In a moment of weakness, he looked to his own efforts and sank. Maybe Jesus named him Peter because he sank like a "rock," which gives new meaning to the term "name-dropping"!

After the resurrection, Jesus asked Simon to "feed my lambs, tend my sheep, and feed my sheep" (John 21:15). Three times he said yes. Jesus forgave him for the three denials. Simon Peter became a courageous and caring shepherd of the church.

Reflections

Jesus is about giving second chances. Peter never hesitated to let others know that he had made mistakes and that Jesus had forgiven him. Mark's Gospel is brutally frank about Peter's failing. This disciple was not perfect, yet Jesus accepted and helped him.

One day Peter asked Jesus, "Lord, if another member of the church sins against me, how often should I forgive? Seven times? Jesus said to him, "Not seven times, but, I tell you, seventy-seven times" (Matthew 18:21-22). Peter certainly offended Jesus more than seven times, but the master forgave him again and again and again.

Simon Peter became a decisive leader in the early church:

• On Pentecost, Peter's sermon converted three thousand people (Acts 2).

• He performed the first miracle (Acts 3:1-26).

• He defended himself (and John) boldly before the temple authorities (Acts 4).

• Peter was an outspoken leader encouraging the early church to welcome God's children from other nations (Acts 10).

• Peter defended Paul and Barnabas' missionary work (Acts 15).

Peter's positions were not always popular. He sought to do the right thing. Peter is the patron saint of pastors and church leaders who strive for positive change in their churches.

Early church traditions reveal Simon Peter and his wife became missionaries and in that capacity traveled to Antioch, Ephesus, Corinth, and even Rome. Tradition suggests that Peter and Paul were martyred by Roman authorities.

Peter's story is a reminder that we all live as both saint and sinner. Our faith falters at times, and yet because Christ has claimed us as his own, we are forgiven and made whole time after time. In our sinking moments, God's Spirit is there to lift us up. In our moments of fear, God's Spirit brings calm and confidence to us. And in those moments when we try to run away from or deny God's purpose for our lives, God's Spirit draws us back and confirms that Jesus has called us to serve.

Reflection Questions

1. Jesus favored everyday people. Edward Mote, a common carpenter, wrote these verses. How do they reflect Simon Peter's faith journey? Yours?

My hope is built on nothing less than Jesus' blood and righteousness.
I dare not trust the sweetest frame, but wholly trust in Jesus' Name.
When darkness seems to hide His face, I rest on His unchanging grace.
In every high and stormy gale, my anchor holds within the veil.
On Christ the solid Rock I stand, all other ground is sinking sand. (1834)

2. Peter's personal story was probably more effective than any sermon he ever preached. What can others learn from your faith journey?

3. Peter persuaded the early church that was made up primarily of Jewish followers of Jesus to accept the Gentiles. Jesus taught him the importance of accepting others. Who needs your acceptance today? What can you do?

38

Judas Iscariot

Read: John 12:1-8

Background

Okay, okay, what does Judas have to do with being a world class Christian? Well sometimes we learn by looking at opposites. Judas was a gifted and trusted disciple who made bad choices. We learn and grow by listening to his story

Judas is always placed last in a list of the disciples. He is described as "Iscariot," which could mean he came from Kerioth, a town in southern Judea. That would make him the only non-Galilean among the twelve disciples.

Judas was with Jesus from the very beginning. He was there at the wedding in Cana when Jesus turned water into wine. He saw his master feed five thousand people from five loaves of bread and two fishes. He witnessed a lame man walk and a blind man see. He was present when Jesus commanded Lazarus to rise from the dead.

Judas was never treated as an outsider during Jesus' ministry. He held a position of prominence and trust as the group's treasurer. So why did he betray Jesus? Here are a few possibilities:

1. Judas may have tried to force Jesus' hand. The name *Iscariot* could also refer to the "Sicarii," a Zealot partisan group opposed to the Roman government. This group challenged the Roman army at Masada forty years later. Possibly Judas was looking for a messiah like King David. Judas may have misunderstood Jesus' teachings about God's kingdom and simply missed the big picture.

2. Judas may have been greedy. Admittedly, thirty pieces of silver was not a great sum. John states that Judas was a thief who regularly stole from the group's treasury (John 12:6). Such acts were small bounty for betraying the world's greatest treasure.

3. Judas may have been jealous of others. John was the "beloved disciple." Peter, James, and John enjoyed special treatment. Jesus offered Judas honor and respect during the Last Supper (John 13:22-26). Judas was not satisfied. He left the meal early to betray his master.

Judas had difficulty understanding the extravagance of God's grace:

• When Mary anointed Jesus' feet with expensive ointments, Judas complained of the great cost (John 12:3-6).

• Jesus knew Judas' transgressions and yet he lovingly called him, taught him, fed him, cleansed him, and even forgave him from the cross.

• Ironically, Judas was the only disciple to call Jesus "rabbi" in Matthew's Gospel. Judas called Jesus his master but did not follow him.

Reflections

Judas's betrayal earned him the scorn of history. All four gospels vilify him. Dante's *Inferno* states that the lowest levels of hell are reserved for those who are traitors to family, traitors to country, murderers of invited guests, and traitors to God (including Lucifer and Judas). We will never know Judas' true motivations. We do know he followed his own agenda and failed to follow Christ. He missed important teachings of the master:

• Jesus shared with his disciples the "Great Commandment" (John 13:31-35). Jesus said to love each other as God has loved us.

• Jesus declared that he was "the way, the truth, and the life" (John 14:6). Jesus shared salvation.

• Jesus promised the gift of the Holy Spirit (John 14:15-29), the gift that brings heavenly power and peace.

• Jesus prayed for his disciples (John 17). This prayer, called the High Priestly Prayer, was a special blessing for all who follow Jesus.

The name *Judas* actually means one who is "praised" or "celebrated." Unfortunately, he did not live up to his good name. He only praised Jesus on his terms. The church sometimes has more to fear from insiders than from outsiders. Judas was the enemy from within. We should never lose sight of the fact that this is never our church. This is forever Christ's church.

Responsible Christians do not concentrate on themselves but on what God wants them to do. We openly pray the words "thy will be done on earth as it is in heaven" in the Lord's Prayer. These words commit us to seeking the will of God and then doing it. The "Judas" attitude seems always to end with "no" and is a prime example of seeking "MY" will instead of "THY" will. Still, we can mourn for Judas, because his act of betrayal began the series of events that led Jesus to the cross. And it is at the cross that Jesus won salvation for all who believe.

Reflection Questions

1. Richard of Chichester openly fought greed with a vow of poverty. He was known as the barefoot bishop who unselfishly cared for his flock. Consider his verses. Who should be first in our lives? How should we follow?

Day by day, dear Lord, of thee three things I pray:
To see thee more clearly, love thee more dearly,
Follow thee more nearly, day by day. (1197-1253)

2. What can we do to help others have a closer walk with God?

3. How can we always seek to please God and not just ourselves?

39

Timothy

Read: Philippians 1:1-11

Background

The fact that Timothy was Paul's special companion and assistant for seventeen years does not make sense. He had too many things going against him. Then again, Timothy's life and ministry are opportunities to see God's glory and grace at work.

Timothy was from the town of Lystra in south central Turkey, a crossroads for travel and commerce. Paul and Barnabas visited the town on their first missionary journey. Paul preached in the market square and healed a lame man. The townspeople were so impressed they said Barnabas was like the god Zeus and Paul was like Hermes. Modern archeology has even uncovered statues of Zeus and Hermes at the front gates of this ancient city.

Paul and Barnabas used the opportunity to witness about the one true God. Troublemakers from a nearby town arrived, and the fickle people of Lystra began to stone Paul and Barnabas. Paul was left for dead (Acts 14), but he recovered. With such an introduction to missionary life, Timothy had no false impressions regarding the cost of discipleship.

Timothy came from a "mixed marriage." His father was a pagan Gentile, and his mother was a Jew. Timothy was not circumcised. This indicates that his mother did not practice her faith. Paul and Barnabas changed all that. Timothy, his mother, and grandmother all became faithful members of the Christian church at Lystra.

Years later, Paul boldly returned to Lystra during his second missionary journey (Acts 16:1-3). Timothy joined him and from that time onward he was Paul's constant companion.

• He was Paul's representative to the churches at Macedonia (Acts 19:22), Thessalonica (1 Thessalonians 1:1), Philippi (Philippians 2:19), and Corinth (1 Corinthians 4:17; 16:10).

• He was with Paul when he wrote his letters to the churches at Thessalonica (1 Thessalonians 1:1; 3:2, 6), Rome (Romans 16:21), Corinth (2 Corinthians 1:1, 19) Colossae (Colossians 1:1), and to Philemon (Philemon 1:1).

• He helped in the collection of charity, which was taken to the starving people in Jerusalem (Acts 20:4).

• He was with Paul in prison when he wrote to the church in Philippi (Philippians 1:1).

Paul's letter to the Corinthians indicates Timothy could be timid or unsure of himself. Paul urged the Corinthians to put Timothy at ease. They were instructed not to mistreat him, and he asked to send Timothy back with their blessings (1 Corinthians 16:10-11).

Paul's later treatment of Timothy was at variance with his behavior toward John Mark. Possibly Paul learned lessons from the struggles in Jerusalem. Paul would have been the first to admit, "God is not finished with me yet." Timothy and Paul helped each other grow. Paul initially called Timothy his "dear and faithful child in the Lord," then "his brother," and finally his "fellow-worker."

Timothy was not a bold and charismatic leader (like Paul), but he did have courage. And as the letters to Timothy in the New Testament indicate, he was a trusted leader of the church at an early age (1 Timothy 4:12). Eusebius, the fourth-century historian and bishop of Caesarea, wrote that Timothy became the bishop of Ephesus. Tradition indicates that he was martyred there for boldly fighting the abuses of women and children in the temple of Artemis. Ultimately this faithful youth became a champion for all God's children.

Reflections

Paul spent his life encouraging new Christians and developing congregations. Often this work was accomplished through letters or personal emissaries. Paul showed us a model of mentoring Timothy to be a partner in ministry.

Mentoring others is an important ministry in the church. Healthy churches should give less experienced members a chance to participate in all congregational ministries. Studies show that new members remain active in church when they are fully engaged. Youth, in particular, often have great gifts of energy, enthusiasm, creativity, and optimism to share in the work of the kingdom. How is your church involving new members and encouraging youth to be active in the ministry of the church?

The name *Timothy* is Greek for "one who honors God." The word *honor* means "a strong commitment to do what is right," "to respect with reverence," "elevation of character," and "divine generosity." Timothy certainly lived up to his namesake. Our purpose in life is to honor God with our worship and with our service.

The service known as the Affirmation of Baptism summarizes our call and our challenge as baptized persons. Each person who has pledged their faith is asked these questions: Do you intend to continue in the covenant God made with you in Holy Baptism:

To live among God's faithful people,

To hear his word and share in his supper,

To proclaim the good news of God in Christ through word and deed,

To serve all people, following the example of our Lord Jesus,

And to strive for justice and peace in all the earth?

(From *Lutheran Book of Worship*, p. 201)

Reflection Questions

1. Martin Luther based this hymn on Psalm 46. He often shared these words with his partners in ministry. Together they found comfort. Who is always by our side? How does Christ win?

A mighty fortress is our God, a bulwark never failing;
Our helper he, amid the flood of mortal ills prevailing.
For still our ancient foe doth seek to work us woe;
His craft and power are great, and, armed with cruel hate,
On earth is not his equal.
Did we in our strength confide, our striving would be losing;
Were not the right Man on our side, the Man of God's own choosing:
Dost ask who that may be? Christ Jesus, it is He;
Lord Sabbaoth, His Name, from age to age the same,
And He must win the battle. (1529)

2. What needs to happen in your church or your family to encourage young people in the faith?

3. Who have you ever mentored in the faith? Who needs your help now?

40

Spirit of God

Read: John 14:15-27

Background

In this passage from John's Gospel, Jesus is preparing his followers to carry on after he is gone. He will send an "Advocate" (the Holy Spirit) to teach them the way of love and the way of truth. As Advocate, the Spirit will walk beside and teach Christ's followers. They will not be left to fend for themselves. The fulfillment of these promises came on the celebration of Pentecost, just a short time after Jesus had ascended into heaven (see Luke 24:50-53 and Acts 2).

The Holy Spirit remains our constant companion and guide in the church. Without the working of the Spirit, the church and its people would not survive. As Martin Luther has said: "The work of the Holy Spirit [is] to reveal through the Gospel and what great glorious things God has done for us through Jesus Christ. . . ."

Reflections

We began this study reflecting God's name. *Yahweh* was with us in the past, is with us now, and will always be with us. This is the God of all creation. God's steadfast love endures forever.

The name *Jesus* means "God is my salvation." It reveals God's abiding care for all of us. Through Jesus we meet God. We are on a first-name basis with God. Knowing Jesus enables us to communicate with God. We are saved from all that separates us from God and from one another.

Throughout this study we have examined people whose lives were affected by Jesus. Some lived up to their namesakes. Others did not. Others received new God-given names when their lives were transformed.

Through the work of the Holy Spirit we are gathered together in God's name. Martin Luther taught, "I believe that by my own reason or strength I cannot believe in Jesus Christ, my Lord, or come to him, but the Holy Spirit has called me through the Gospel, enlightened me with gifts, and sanctified and preserved me in the true faith" (*Small Catechism*).

When we are born is never as important as when we are "born from above." That is the day God names and claims us. Christians are all baptized in "the name of the Father, the Son, and the Holy Spirit." We share the same family name. Our baptisms begin life-long journeys with God and God's people. We need to affirm these same baptisms every day of our lives.

The biblical word for *Spirit* is the same as "breath" or "wind." Jesus refers to the Spirit as the "Paraclete" or "Advocate" (John 14). This is an ancient term describing someone who stands beside you in times of great battle. Christ's Spirit stands besides us through our struggles and times of greatest need. We are never alone.

The Spirit shares with us many special gifts (including faith, peace, hope, joy) that help us on our spiritual journeys. Paul describes the Spirit's greatest gift to us all. "Love is patient; love is kind; . . . It bears all things, believes all things, hopes all things, endures all things . . . And now faith, hope, and love abide, and the greatest of these is love" (1 Corinthians 13).

The work of the Spirit enables us to work together. It helps us affirm our relationship with other Christians and with churches everywhere working together in Christ's name. The Holy Spirit unites us in one mission. One faith. One baptism. One Gospel. One Lord of all!

This is the shortest chapter of this book because we must each write our own ending. Each of us must include our own story as part of this final chapter. The Spirit blesses us with gifts and abilities for the work of the Kingdom. Jesus instructed us to work together for the sake of the Kingdom.

The Spirit is Christ's gift that just keeps on giving every day of our lives. Together we grow in worship, service, outreach, fellowship, and discipleship. Together our lives proclaim, "To God be the Glory." This is most certainly true.

Reflection Questions

1. Abbot Rabanus Maurus (776-856) dedicated his life to building churches (physically and spiritually). How does he describe the work of the Holy Spirit? How can we be "but one"?

Come, Holy Ghost, our souls inspire, ignite them with celestial fire;
Spirit of God, you have the art, your gifts, the sevenfold, to impart.
Your blest outpouring from above is comfort, life, and fire of love.
Illumine with perpetual light, the dullness of our blinded sight.

Anoint and cheer our much-soiled face with the abundance of your grace.
Keep far our foes; give peace at home; where you guide us, no ill can come.
Teach us to know the Father, Son, and you, of both, to be but one
That, as the ceaseless ages throng, your praise may be our endless song!

2. What are new ways that Christian churches can work together? How can we be transparent?

3. What gifts has the Holy Spirit given you to share? What can we do together today? Tomorrow?

4. Consider your life and faith. Write your own personal "purpose" or "mission" statement.